A Farm Journal Craft Book

Knit Sweaters the Easy Way

–using the straight-line method

By Solweig Hedin

Farm Journal, Inc.
Philadelphia, Pennsylvania

Distributed to the trade by
Doubleday & Company, Inc.
Garden City, New York

Other Farm Journal Craft Books

Scrap Saver's Stitchery Book
More Scrap Saver's Stitchery
Let's Make a Patchwork Quilt
Farm Journal's Homespun Christmas
Farm Journal's Design-and-Sew Children's Clothes
Easy Sewing with Knits
Modern Patchwork

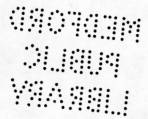
Illustrations: Solweig Hedin
Photos: George Faraghan
Book Design: Michael P. Durning

Library of Congress Cataloging in Publication Data

Hedin, Solweig
　Knit sweaters the easy way
　—using the straight-line method.

　(A Farm journal craft book)
　Includes index.
　1. Sweaters. I. Title. II. Series.
TT825.H4　746.9'2　8l-5425
ISBN　0-385-15515-8　AACR2

contents

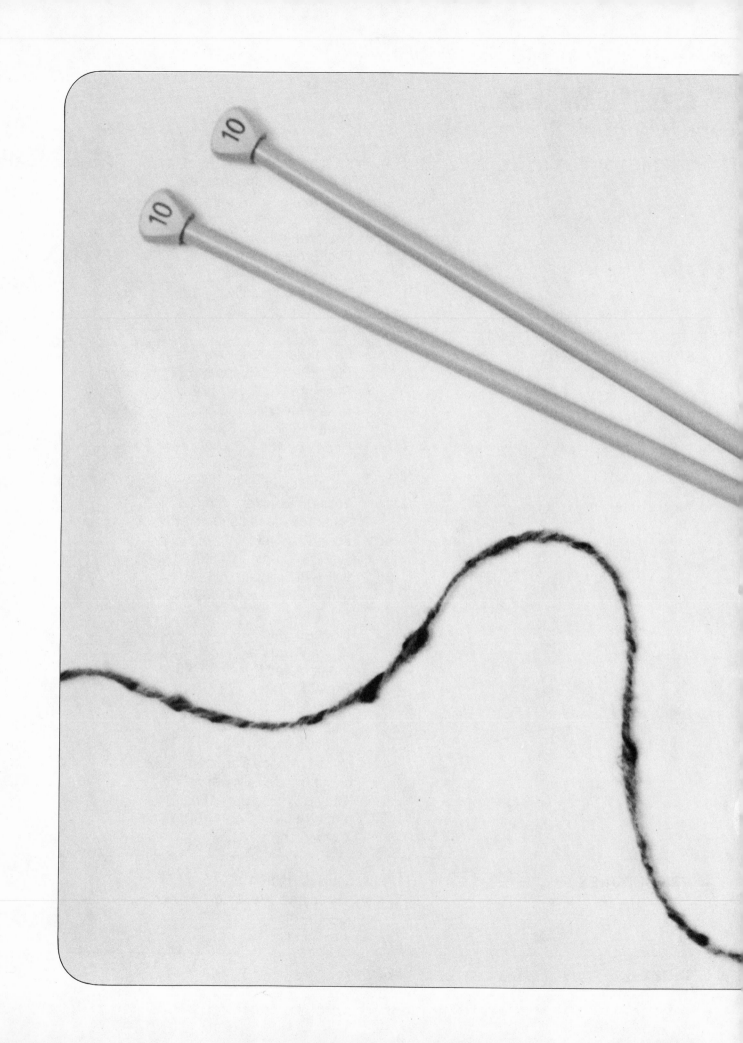

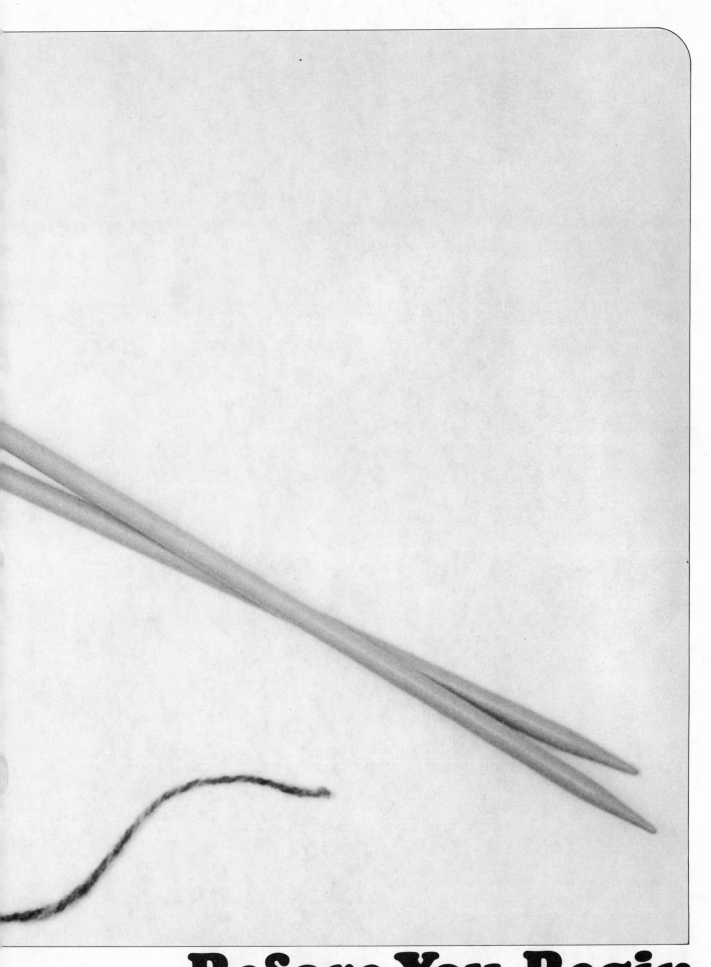

Before You Begin

knitting

One of the oldest and most unique crafts, knitting has been virtually untouched by modern inventions. Needles (the tools) have been made lighter over the years. Yarns (the medium) are more interesting and varied in both texture and color. But the technique remains the same. You still use only two needles, a ball of yarn, and two basic stitches—Knit and Purl.

The multitude of pattern variations derived from these two stitches has made knitting one of the most versatile crafts. People of different countries have contributed their own stitch patterns, reflecting their folk art, traditions and designs. These patterns have been handed down and added to through generations. With such a heritage, knitting continues to be a source of infinite possibilities and inspiration.

The craft of knitting goes back to the beginnings of civilization. During the Middle Ages, knitting flourished as a highly refined craft with its own guild. To qualify as a member, a man (never a woman) had to work as an apprentice to a master for several years, study for several more, and then produce original masterpieces of his own.

Today the knitter doesn't have to go through such an elaborate process. Even so, there still is no such thing as "instant knitting." It takes practice and patience to gain the skill needed to create that special masterpiece, but it is well worth the time and effort. The beautifully designed, skillfully executed hand-knitted sweater will never lose its character, nor will it fall from favor or go out of style.

the straight-line shape

Every sweater in this book, whether narrow or loose in style, is based on the same simple shape.

I have taken an age-old, straight-line pattern used for making a garment. This basic shape, combined with the knitting technique and adapted to modern style and materials, becomes a blueprint for the creation of a hand-knitted garment.

My master plan has been to simplify both the shaping and the knitting instructions, without sacrificing good fit. With the basic shape, no increases or decreases are made along the edges (except in a few cases).

The armhole/sleeve construction is especially important. Sleeves are worked directly onto the sweater by picking up the stitches along the armhole edges. This eliminates the tedious job of setting in the sleeves, as well as the bulkiness of a conventional seam. In addition, sleeves can be narrow without sacrificing comfortable armhole space. Or armholes and sleeves can be extra-large and still retain the good shoulder fit.

This basic shape has many design possibilities. Without changing the armhole/sleeve construction, you can make anything from a short-sleeve sweater top to a bulky coat. The finished work is a well-made, beautifully fitting sweater that conforms to the natural lines of the body.

stitches & yarns

The two basic stitches—Knit and Purl—alone have enough variations to last the knitter a lifetime. What other craft has such richness?

All the pattern stitches used for the garments in this book are easy to work. I have intentionally avoided complicated and lengthy patterns, as well as ''plain'' knitting. Instead, I have selected simple pattern stitches that are decorative either by themselves or combined with each other.

But stitches alone do not make the sweater. An equally important factor is the knitting yarn. There are many different types and qualities available, and these come in a wide range of beautiful colors. I have selected yarns that should be easy to find in a well-stocked yarn shop. If a particular yarn is not in stock, often the shop will order it for you.

Other yarns besides those specified can

be used, of course (see substituting yarns, below, and test swatch, pg. 8). Since the knitted garment is also a fashion item, many interesting "seasonal" or novelty yarns and colors are available. The standard types—fingering yarn, sport-weight yarn and knitting worsted—will continue season after season, but colors will change.

As a rule, working with an excellent quality yarn will result in a long-lasting finished project that you will be proud of, even if you are an inexperienced knitter and your stitches are uneven. On the other hand, a perfectly made sweater can be flat, uninteresting and short-lasting if the yarn that you use is inferior.

SUBSTITUTING YARNS: When substituting a yarn, there are two important factors to consider—the stitch gauge and the fiber content of the yarn.

Accuracy of the stitch gauge is crucial. If you are working with an incorrect gauge, it will be necessary to make adjustments (see test swatch, pg. 8). In some cases, if the gauge of the new yarn is larger or smaller, it might be possible to simply follow instructions for a smaller or larger size to get the correct measurements. If the sweater style is loose and the "new" gauge will make it only slightly larger or smaller, the difference in gauge may not be important.

Always remember—a small difference in the gauge may make a big difference in the overall measurement.

The content of the new yarn can be different, but then the finished garment may also look different. A quality wool-blend yarn is easily exchanged with a quality wool, or vice versa. However, a garment made of soft pure wool will both look and "behave" differently from one made in a cotton or a synthetic yarn. Pattern stitches will look different, too, because the "bounce" of most wool cannot be found in cotton or synthetic yarn (see test swatch, pg. 8).

As a rule, the stitch gauge of the substituted yarn should be the same as the stitch gauge in the instructions. The fiber content of the new yarn should be as close as possible to the one suggested if you want the same look. A well-stocked yarn shop should have an up-to-date yarn chart which compares most brand names and types of yarn.

COLORS: Color choices are very personal, and color, as well as stitch combinations, can be the signature of the knitter. No fancy stitch can compete with a quality yarn in a beautiful color worked in the simple Garter Stitch. And a "crazy" color combination will always be a conversation piece.

As a rule, dark colors will not show pattern stitches as well as light colors. A multicolored, textured yarn needs a simple stitch to bring out the interesting look of the yarn. An intricate stitch will be lost in a novelty yarn.

It is the combinations of pattern stitches, yarns, and colors that give hand knitting the look of creative originality.

tools

- Knitting needles in several sizes.
- Circular needles for working a turtleneck, neckband or front bands.
- A stitch holder for making a cable.
- A crochet hook for picking up stitches or finishing an edge.
- A pair of scissors for cutting yarn.
- A tapestry needle for weaving in yarn ends.
- A cork to prevent stitches from slipping off needle when not in use.
- Large safety pins for holding stitches.
- A pad and a pencil for making notes.

KNITTING NEEDLES: Many sweater designs require needles in two or more different sizes. The bottom ribbing, the sleeve cuffs and the neckband usually are worked on needles smaller than those used for the rest of the garment. Different size needles also are required when working a combination of pattern stitches in different gauges, or when working with a combination of yarns in different thicknesses.

To change needles while working, transfer stitches to new size needle by simply working stitches off the old needle onto the new size. Then continue working with both new needles.

KNITTING NEEDLE SIZES

American	Metric (mm)
00	2
0	2.25
1	2.5
2	2.75
3	3.25
4	3.5
5	3.75
6	4
7	4.5
8	5
9	5.5
10	6
10½	6.5
11	7
-	7.5
13	8
15	8.5

CROCHET HOOK SIZES

American	Metric (mm)
B	2
C	2.5
D	3
E	3.5
F	4
G	4.5
H	5
I	5.5
J	6
-	6.5
K	7

test swatch

A must for every knitter! To a new knitter, a swatch may at first seem both time-consuming and boring. But this step is very important. It will save you time and trouble later when working on your actual project.

It is also here—by working up swatches—that individual taste and creativity can be turned into some very personal and unusual knits. An original can be created by interchanging designs (taking part of a design from one sweater and using it in another); by testing and combining various pattern stitches with different weight yarns; by adding a new yarn to a design; or by working in a different gauge.

Most instructions in this book give both stitch and row gauge. The stitch gauge is the more important and should always be followed. The row gauge is only indicated when rows can easily be counted. It is useful information when you are planning a project where row measurement is important to the design, or when you are counting rows instead of inches while knitting.

If your row gauge is slightly off from that in the instructions, the finished garment will be either longer or shorter. For example, a design may have repeats of stripes or pattern shapes that should be completed, and a different row gauge will change the length measurement. However, a small variation in length might not be important.

To make a test swatch:

First—After selecting yarn, pattern stitch and needles, work up a swatch no less than 4 inches square. This first step is to learn how to work the stitch. If you are working in a different yarn, you will also find out how the pattern stitch, combined with the new yarn, looks and feels. Write down any personal notes that can be helpful.

Second—Check to see that the pattern stitch is worked correctly and evenly. Measure the gauge of the unblocked swatch, making sure that it is not being pulled.

Third—Compare the gauge of the swatch with the gauge in the instructions. If your gauge is larger, try to work tighter, or the finished garment will be larger than the size in the instructions. If your gauge is smaller, work looser, or the garment will end up smaller. If the result still is not satisfactory, change needles; use a smaller size if your gauge is too large, and a larger size if your gauge is too small.

As a rule, stitches should be firmly wrapped around the needle, but still easy to remove.

Fourth—With everything checked and rechecked (especially important if creating a new design), it is now time to start your knitting project. Always keep the swatch and notes nearby, and save them for future reference and inspiration.

Note: If the desired effect is a very loosely knitted garment, be sure that the yarn doesn't have too much "give," especially when worked on extra-large needles. A 100% synthetic yarn doesn't have the "bounce back" of a pure wool; it has a tendency to get out—and stay out—of shape if knitted loosely or on too-large needles. Cotton, linen and silk yarns also have very little elasticity and will stretch to a degree. Try to avoid using them with pattern stitches that are too open and "lacy."

first project

Many new knitters feel that because they are inexperienced, it doesn't matter what yarn they use for their first project. Not so at all! I can't stress enough the importance of good working materials. Starting off with an uninspiring color and a lifeless-looking yarn can only result in disinterest for this fun and enriching craft.

Choose a quality, medium-weight yarn in a favorite color to use with a simple design. Large needles and a thick yarn work up faster, but not necessarily easier, than fine needles and a fine yarn. Big needles can be, at times, as difficult to handle as very fine needles. Thick, bulky yarn can be difficult to work with when you are learning the basic stitches.

garment sizing

Measurements for all garments in this book are based on standard sizing (see chart, next page). The size of a finished garment is also based on style. A loosely fitted sweater may appear to have measurements that belong to a larger size when extra inches are added to the width, length and armhole. The garment retains its good fit, however, because measurements for the neckline and sleeve length remain in the smaller size.

Group sizing is used in the instructions, and garment measurements are based on the larger size within each group.

designing your own

After the selected pattern stitch and yarn are worked into a test swatch, you must determine personal garment measurements.

First—Take your body measurements or use those listed under standard sizing, next page, then check guidelines for sizing a garment, pg. 12.

Second—Make up a garment diagram (page 12) and indicate required measurements.

Third—Determine the number of stitches needed by multiplying the width of the garment by the stitch gauge. If the width is 18 inches and there are 20 stitches to 4 inches (5 stitches to one inch), multiply 18 inches by 5 stitches (for a total of 90 stitches).

Next, divide the total number of stitches by the number of stitches in the pattern stitch repeat—and add 2 edge stitches (see edge stitches, pg. 116). For example, the Trinity Stitch is worked over 4 stitches, plus 2 stitches (not counting the 2 edge stitches). Thus, 90 stitches divided by 4 = 22 repeats of 4 stitches, plus 2 stitches extra. You can work the pattern stitch, using the 2 extra stitches as edge stitches—or you can add 2 edge stitches.

If a more intricate pattern stitch is used, either add or subtract stitches so that the

STANDARD SIZING
(with body measurements)

WOMEN

Size:		6-8	10-12	14-16	18
Bust:	in.	30½-31½	32½-34	36-38	40
	(cm)	(77.5-80)	(82.5-86.5)	(91.5-96.5)	(101.5)
Half Bust Size:	in.	15¼-15¾	16¼-17	18-19	20
	(cm)	(38.5-40)	(41.25-43.25)	(45.75-48.25)	(50.75)
Hip:	in.	32½-33½	34½-36	38-40	42
	(cm)	(82.5-85)	(87.5-91.5)	(96.5-101.5)	(106.5)
Sleeve Length:	in.	16¾	17-17½	17¾-18	18½
	(cm)	(42.5)	(43-44.5)	(45-45.5)	(47)
Wrist:	in.	6	6¼	6½	6½
	(cm)	(15)	(16)	(16.5)	(16.5)

MEN

Size:		34-36	38-40	42-44	46-48
Chest:	in.	34-36	38-40	42-44	46-48
	(cm)	(86.5-91.5)	(96.5-101.5)	(106.5-112)	(117-122)
Half Chest Size:	in.	17-18	19-20	21-22	23-24
	(cm)	(43.25-45.75)	(48.25-50.75)	(53.25-56)	(58.5-61)
Hip:	in.	35-37	39-41	43-45	47-49
	(cm)	(89-94)	(99-104)	(109-114.5)	(119.5-124.5)
Sleeve Length:	in.	17½-18	18½-19	19½-20	20-20½
	(cm)	(44.5-45.5)	(47-48)	(49.5-51)	(51-52)
Wrist:	in.	6¾	7	7¼	7½
	(cm)	(17)	(18)	(18.5)	(19)

CHILDREN

Size:		3-4	5-6	7-8	10-12
Chest:	in.	22-23	24-25	26-27	28½-30
	(cm)	(56-58.5)	(61-63.5)	(66-68.5)	(72.5-76)
Half Chest Size:	in.	11-11½	12-12½	13-13½	14¼-15
	(cm)	(28-29.25)	(30.5-31.75)	(33-34.25)	(36.25-38)
Hip:	in.	23-24	25-26	27-28	30-32
	(cm)	(58.5-61)	(63.5-66)	(68.5-71)	(76-81)
Sleeve Length:	in.	9½-10½	11-11½	12-12½	13½-15
	(cm)	(24-26.5)	(28-29)	(30.5-31.5)	(34.5-38)
Wrist:	in.	5¼	5½	5¾	6
	(cm)	(13.5)	(14)	(14.5)	(15)

Note: The metric equivalents to inches are approximate.

11

pattern stitch will come out even—or make the necessary adjustments between repeats or at the sides.

The same principle is used when working out a pattern stitch for the sleeves.

GUIDELINES FOR SIZING A GARMENT: The measurements indicated below should be used to work out the size of a garment.

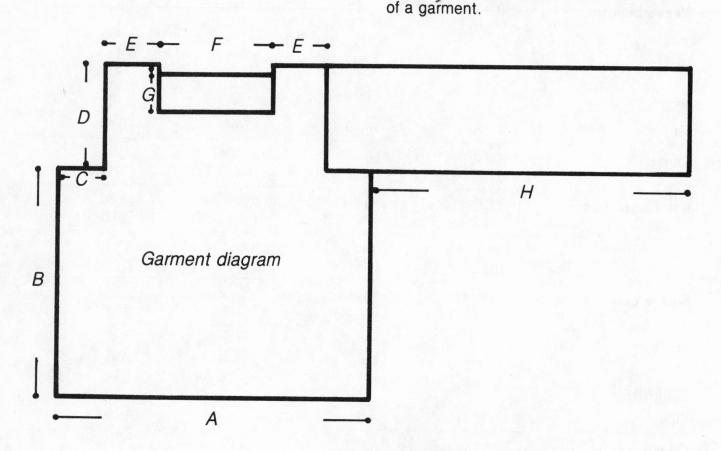

Garment diagram

A. Width Back & Front (based on half-bust or half-chest size, or on style).
B. Length (based on style).
C. Armhole width (based on style).
D. Armhole length (based on upper arm size and style).
E. Shoulder width (based on style).
F. Neckline width (based on standard sizing and style).
G. Neckline depth (based on style).
H. Sleeve length (based on standard sizing and style).

Width of garment—For a fitted garment, add 1-1½ in. (2.5-4 cm) to half-bust or half-chest measurement (see standard sizing chart). For a loose style, add 2-2½ in. (5-6 cm), and for a very loose style, add 3-3½ in. (7.5-9 cm).

Armhole—The armhole measurement (see pg. 14) is based on the standard upper arm circumference measurement. This is a *minimum* measurement that will give a fitted armhole and a narrow sleeve when the garment is worked in a light- to medium-weight yarn. As a rule, add 1¾-2 in. (4.5-5 cm) to upper arm circumference. If working in a heavy yarn, add an additional ½ in. (1.25 cm) to Back and Front armhole length for a *minimum* measurement.

Neckline—The neckline measurement (see pg. 14) is an *average* size for working a crew neck, neckband or turtleneck.

SWEATER MEASUREMENTS
FOR ARMHOLE & NECKLINE

WOMEN

Size:		6-8	10-12	14-16	18
Armhole:	in. (cm)	11½ (29)	12-12½ (30.5-32)	13-13½ (33-34.5)	14 (35.5)
Half Armhole:	in. (cm)	5¾ (14.5)	6-6¼ (15.25-16)	6½-6¾ (16.5-17.25)	7 (17.75)
Neckline Width:	in. (cm)	5¼ to 5¾ (13.5 to 14.5)	5¾ to 6¼ (14.5 to 16)	6¼ to 6¾ (16 to 17)	6¾ to 7¼ (17 to 18.5)

MEN

Size:		34-36	38-40	42-44	46-48
Armhole:	in. (cm)	15½-16 (39.5-40.5)	16½-17 (42-43)	17½-18 (44.5-46)	18½-19 (47-48)
Half Armhole:	in. (cm)	7¾-8 (19.75-20.25)	8¼-8½ (21-21.5)	8¾-9 (22.25-23)	9¼-9½ (23.5-24)
Neckline Width:	in. (cm)	6¼ to 6½ (16 to 16.5)	6¾ to 7 (17 to 18)	7¼ to 7½ (18.5 to 19)	7¾ to 8 (19.5 to 20.5)

CHILDREN

Size:		3-4	5-6	7-8	10-12
Armhole:	in. (cm)	8-8½ (20.5-21.5)	9-9½ (23-24)	10-10½ (25.5-26.7)	11-11½ (28-29)
Half Armhole:	in. (cm)	4-4½ (10.25-10.75)	4½-4¾ (11.5-12)	5-5¼ (12.75-13.25)	5½-5¾ (14-14.5)
Neckline Width:	in. (cm)	4¼ to 4½ (11 to 11.5)	4½ to 4¾ (11.5 to 12)	4¾ to 5 (12 to 12.5)	5 to 5¼ (12.5 to 13.5)

Note: The metric equivalents to inches are approximate.

abbreviations

beg	begin
cm	centimeter(s)
dec	decrease
gr	gram(s)
in.	inch(es)
inc	increase
incl.	including
m	meter(s)
mm	millimeter(s)
oz.	ounce(s)
psso	pass slipped stitch over
rep	repeat
—	repeat from * to *
st	stitch
sts	stitches
tog	together
yo	yarn over needle

Sweaters to Knit

fisherman's knit

This traditional pure wool pullover is a combination of pattern stitches. It may look intricate, but because each pattern stitch is worked in its own vertical panel, the knitting turns out to be easy.

(color photo, page 31)

SIZES: 6-8 / 10-12 / 14-16 / 18
For standard sizing, see pg. 11.

MATERIALS: Chanteleine ''Tipshet''
(100% wool), imported by Merino
Wool. Ecru—13/14/14/15 skeins
@ 1¾ oz. (50 gr) per skein.
Knitting needles size 8 (5 mm) and
size 10 (6 mm).
Circular needle size 8 (5 mm).

GAUGE: Pattern Stitches and size 10
needles, 16 stitches = 4 in.
(10 cm).

STITCHES USED: For abbreviations,
see pg. 15. For how to knit, see
pg. 108.

Tunisian Stitch_____
Worked over 2 stitches plus 1.
Row 1 (wrong side): Knit 1, *Yo, Slip 1,
Knit 1*. Repeat *—*.
Row 2: *Knit 1, Twist Knit 2 together (Yo
and Slip Stitch)*. Repeat *—*:
Knit 1.
Repeat rows 1, 2.
Note: All Slip Stitches are slipped purlwise
with yarn in back.

Broken Single Rib_____
Row 1 (wrong side): *Knit 1, Purl 1*.
Repeat *—*.
Row 2: Purl across.
Repeat rows 1, 2.

Single Rib_____
Worked over 2 stitches.
Row 1: *Knit 1, Purl 1*. Repeat *—*.
Row 2: *Knit 1, Purl 1*. Repeat *—*.
Repeat rows 1, 2.

Plait Cable_____
Worked over 9 stitches plus 4.

Row 1 (right side): Purl 2, Knit 9, Purl 2.
Row 2: Knit 2, Purl 9, Knit 2.
Row 3: Purl 2, Slip 3 stitches onto cable
   needle and leave in front, Knit 3,
   Knit 3 from cable needle, Knit 3,
   Purl 2.
Row 4: Knit 2, Purl 9, Knit 2.
Row 5: Purl 2, Knit 9, Purl 2.
Row 6: Knit 2, Purl 9, Knit 2.
Row 7: Purl 2, Knit 3, Slip 3 stitches onto
   cable needle and leave in back,
   Knit 3, Knit 3 from cable needle,
   Purl 2.
Row 8: Knit 2, Purl 9, Knit 2.
   Repeat rows 1-8.

Trinity Stitch

Worked over 4 stitches plus 2.
Row 1 (wrong side): Knit 1, *Knit 1/Purl 1/
   Knit 1 into one stitch, Purl 3 to-
   gether*. Repeat *—*. Knit 1.
Row 2: Purl across.
Row 3: Knit 1, *Purl 3 together, Knit 1/
   Purl 1/Knit 1 into one stitch*.
   Repeat *—*. Knit 1.
Row 4: Purl across.
   Repeat rows 1-4.

Note: Edge stitches are not included in
   stitch instructions, above. See
   edge stitches, pg. 116.

BACK: With size 8 needles, Cast On
67/71/79/83 sts. Work Tunisian Stitch for
3½ in. (9 cm).
Stockinette Stitch—Change to size 10
needles.
Row 1 (right side): Knit across and Inc 8
sts. Inc 1 st on each side edge, remaining
6 sts evenly across.
Row 2: Knit 1 (edge st), Purl 73/77/85/89,
Knit 1 (edge st).
Pattern Stitches—
First row worked is row 2 of Broken Rib,
row 4 of Trinity Stitch and row 1 of Cable.
Row 1 (right side): Knit 1 (edge st). Broken
Rib—Purl 11/13/15/17. Rib—Knit
2/2/3/3. Trinity—Purl 15. Rib—Knit
2/2/3/3. Cable—Purl 2, Knit 9, Purl 2.

Rib—Knit 2/2/3/3. Trinity—Purl 15.
Rib—Knit 2/2/3/3. Broken Rib—Purl
11/13/15/17. Knit 1 (edge st).
Row 2: Knit 1. Broken Rib—*Knit 1,
Purl 1*. Rep *—*4/5/6/7 more times.
Knit 1. Rib—Purl 2/2/3/3. Trinity—Knit 1,
Knit/Purl/Knit into one stitch, Purl 3 tog.
Rep *—* 2 more times. Knit/Purl/Knit into
one stitch, Knit 1. Rib—Purl 2/2/3/3.
Cable—Knit 2, Purl 9, Knit 2. Rib—Purl
2/2/3/3. Trinity—Knit 1, *Knit/Purl/Knit in-
to one stitch, Purl 3 tog*. Rep *—* 2 more
times. Knit/Purl/Knit into one stitch.
Rib—Purl 2/2/3/3. Broken Rib—*Knit 1,
Purl 1*. Rep *—* 4/5/6/7 more times.
Knit 2.
Row 3: Knit 1. Broken Rib—Purl
11/13/15/17. Rib—Knit 2/2/3/3. Trini-
ty—Purl 17. Rib—Knit 2/2/3/3. Cable—
Purl 2, Slip 3 sts onto cable needle and
leave in front, Knit 3, Knit 3 from cable nee-
dle, Knit 3, Purl 2. Rib—Knit 2/2/3/3. Trini-
ty—Purl 17. Rib—Knit 2/2/3/3. Broken
Rib—Purl 11/13/15/17. Knit 1.
Row 4: Knit 1. Broken Rib—*Knit 1,
Purl 1*. Rep *—* 4/5/6/7 more times.
Knit 1. Rib—Purl 2/2/3/3. Trinity—Knit 1,
Purl 3 tog, Knit/Purl/Knit into one stitch.
Rep *—* 2 more times. Purl 3 tog, Knit 1.
Rib—Purl 2/2/3/3. Cable—Knit 2, Purl 9,
Knit 2. Rib—Purl 2/2/3/3. Trinity—Knit 1,
Purl 3 tog, Knit/Purl/Knit into one stitch.
Rep *—* 2 more times. Purl 3 tog, Knit 1.
Rib—Purl 2/2/3/3. Broken Rib—*Knit 1,
Purl 1*. Rep *—* 4/5/6/7 more times.
Knit 2.
Continue working rows 1, 2 of Broken Rib,
rows 1-4 of Trinity Stitch and rows 1-8 of
Cable. Work for 11 in. (28 cm), or work to
desired length.
Armholes (right side): Bind Off in Purl 11
sts. Work pattern 53/57/65/69 sts (incl.
bind off st). Bind Off remaining 11 sts. Cut
yarn. Attach yarn and start next row.
Continue to work pattern for 5½/6/6½/
6¾ in. (14/15.5/16.5/17 cm).
Neck (right side): Cable row 5 or 1—Work
pattern for 13/15/18/19 sts. Bind Off in
Purl 27/27/29/31 sts. Work remaining

13/15/18/19 sts (incl. bind off st).
Shoulders (both stay on needle, but are worked separately): Work pattern for 1 in. (2.5 cm). From right side, Bind Off in Purl.

FRONT: Work same as Back as far as armholes, plus 4½/5/5½/5¾ in. (11.5/12.5/14/14.5 cm).
Neck: Work same as Back.
Shoulders: Work pattern for 2 in. (5 cm), to match Back armhole length.

SHOULDER JOININGS: See pg. 121.

SLEEVES: From right side and on size 10 needle, Pick Up 65/69/73/77 sts (32/34/36/38 sts on each side, plus 1 st from shoulder seam).
Row 1 (wrong side): Knit 1 (edge st), Purl 63/67/71/75, Knit 1 (edge st).
Trinity Stitch & Cable Pattern—
Row 1 (right side): Knit 1, Purl 23/25/27/29, Knit 2, Purl 2, Knit 9, Purl 2, Knit 2, Purl 23/25/27/29, Knit 1.
Row 2: Knit 2/1/2/1, *Knit/Purl/Knit into one stitch, Purl 3 tog*. Rep *—* 4/5/5/6 more times. Knit 2/1/2/1, Purl 2, Knit 2, Purl 9, Knit 2, Purl 2, Knit 2/1/2/1, *Purl 3 tog, Knit/Purl/Knit into one stitch*. Rep *—* 4/5/5/6 more times. Knit 2/1/2/1.
Row 3: Knit 1, Purl 23/25/27/29, Knit 2.

Cable—row 7 for right sleeve, row 3 for left sleeve (see stitch instructions). Knit 2, Purl 23/25/27/29, Knit 1.
Row 4: Knit 2/1/2/1, *Purl 3 tog, Knit/Purl/Knit into one stitch*. Rep *—* 4/5/5/6 more times. Knit 2/1/2/1, Purl 2, Knit 2, Purl 9, Knit 2, Purl 2, Knit 2/1/2/1, *Knit/Purl/Knit into one stitch, Purl 3 tog*. Rep *—* 4/5/5/6 more times. Knit 2/1/2/1.
Continue working rows 1-4 of Trinity Stitch and rows 1-8 of Cable until sleeve length is 14½/15/15½/16 in. (37/38/39.5/40.5 cm), or work to desired length. End by working rows 1 and 5 of Cable.
Cuffs (right side): Change to size 8 needles.
Row 1: Knit and Dec 18/20/20/24 sts evenly across (31/33/37/37 sts remain). Work Tunisian Stitch for 2½ in. (6.5 cm). From wrong side, Bind Off in Chain Knit.

BLOCKING & PRESSING:
See pg 120.

SEAM JOININGS: See pg 121.

NECKBAND: From right side, Pick Up 88/88/92/94 sts around neckline. Place on circular needle. Work Single Rib for 1½ in. (4 cm). From right side, Bind Off in Ribbing.

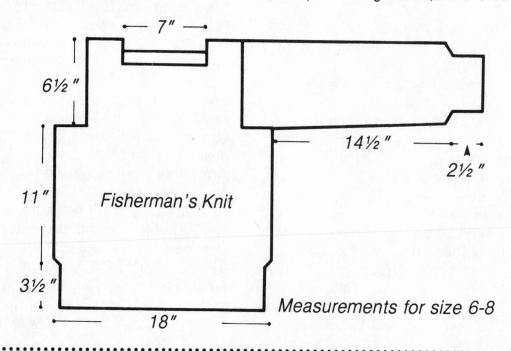

Fisherman's Knit

Measurements for size 6-8

block pattern pullover

Two yarns—of different blends and shades—are combined for a warm and handsome heather effect. A Stockinette Stitch creates the block pattern on the body and sleeves, and the upper section of the body is worked in a Seed Stitch.

(color photo, page 30)

SIZES: 36-38 / 40-42 / 44-46
For standard sizing, see pg. 11.

MATERIALS: Phildar ''Pegase'' (80% acrylic, 20% wool). Dk. Taupe—14/15/16 skeins @ 1¾ oz. (50 gr) per skein.
Phildar ''Anouchka'' (80% acrylic, 16% mohair, 4% wool). Taupe—7/7/8 skeins @ 1²/₅ oz. (40 gr) per skein.
Knitting needles size 8 (5 mm), size 9 (5.5 mm) and size 10 (6 mm).
Circular needle size 8 (5 mm).

GAUGE: Seed Stitch with 2 strands and size 9 needles, 16 stitches and 24 rows = 4 in. (10 cm) square.

STITCHES USED: For abbreviations, see pg. 15. For how to knit, see pg. 108.

Double Rib_____
Worked over 4 stitches plus 2.
Row 1 (wrong side): *Purl 2, Knit 2*. Repeat *—*. Purl 2.
Row 2: *Knit 2, Purl 2*. Repeat *—*. Knit 2.
Repeat rows 1, 2.

Single Rib_____
Worked over 2 stitches.
Row 1: *Knit 1, Purl 1*. Repeat *—*.
Row 2: *Knit 1, Purl 1*. Repeat *—*.
Repeat rows 1, 2.

Block Pattern

Worked over 10 stitches.
Row 1: *Knit 5, Purl 5*. Repeat *—*.
Row 2: *Knit 5, Purl 5*. Repeat *—*.
    Repeat rows 1, 2 twice.
Row 7: Knit across.
Row 8: Purl across.
Row 9: Same as row 2.
Row 10: Same as row 1.
    Repeat rows 9, 10 twice.
Row 15: Same as row 7.
Row 16: Same as row 8.
    Repeat rows 1-16.

Seed Stitch

Worked over 2 stitches.
Row 1: *Knit 1, Purl 1*. Repeat *—*.
Row 2: *Purl 1, Knit 1*. Repeat *—*.
    Repeat rows 1, 2.

Note: Work with 2 strands of yarn throughout (1 strand of each yarn).

BACK: With size 8 needles, Cast On 82/90/94 sts. Work Double Rib for 3½ in. (9 cm).
Stockinette Stitch—
Row 1 (right side): Change to size 10 needles. Knit across and Inc 5/7/8 sts. Inc 1 st on each edge, remaining 3/5/6 sts evenly across.
Row 2: Knit 1 (edge st), Purl 85/95/100, Knit 1 (edge st).
Block Pattern—
Sizes 36-38 & 40-42—
Row 1 (right side): Knit 6, *Purl 5, Knit 5*. Rep *—* 6/7 more times. Purl 5, Knit 6.
Row 2: Knit 1, *Purl 5, Knit 5*. Rep *—* 7/8 more times. Purl 5, Knit 1.
Rep rows 1, 2 two more times.
Size 44-46—
Row 1 (right side): Knit 6, *Purl 5, Knit 5*. Rep *—* 8 more times. Purl 5, Knit 1.
Row 2: Knit 6, *Purl 5, Knit 5*. Rep *—* 8 more times. Purl 5, Knit 1.
Rep rows 1, 2 two more times.
Sizes 36-38 & 40-42 & 44-46—
Row 7: Knit across.

Row 8: Knit 1, Purl 85/95/100, Knit 1.
Sizes 36-38 & 40-42—
Row 9: Knit 1, *Purl 5, Knit 5*. Rep *—* 7/8 more times. Purl 5, Knit 1.
Row 10: Knit 6, *Purl 5, Knit 5*. Rep *—* 6/7 more times. Purl 5, Knit 6.
Rep rows 9, 10 two more times.
Size 44-46—
Row 9: Knit 6, *Purl 5, Knit 5*. Rep *—* 8 more times. Purl 5, Knit 1.
Row 10: Knit 6, *Purl 5, Knit 5*. Rep *—* 8 more times. Purl 5, Knit 1.
Rep rows 9, 10 two more times.
Sizes 36-38 & 40-42 & 44-46—
Row 15: Knit across.
Row 16: Knit 1, Purl 85/95/100, Knit 1.
Rep rows 1-16 four more times. Block Pattern measures 14 in. (35.5 cm). Or work to desired length.
Seed Stitch—
Change to size 9 needles and work Seed Stitch for 8 rows.
Armholes: From right side, Bind Off in Knit 10/11/12 sts. Work pattern 67/75/78 sts (incl. bind off st). Bind Off remaining 10/11/12 sts. Cut yarns. Attach yarns and start next row.
Continue working for 7½/8/8½ in. (19/20.5/22 cm).
Neck (right side): Work pattern 19/22/23 sts. Bind Off in Knit 29/31/32 sts. Work remaining 19/22/23 sts (incl. bind off st).
Shoulders (both stay on needle, but are worked separately): Work pattern for 5 more rows. From right side, Bind Off in Knit.

FRONT: Work same as Back as far as armholes, plus 6½/7/7½ in. (16.5/18/19 cm).
Neck (right side): Work same as Back.
Shoulders: Work pattern for 11 rows, or work to match Back. From right side, Bind Off in Knit.

SHOULDER JOININGS: See pg. 121.

SLEEVES: From right side and on size 10 needle, Pick Up 67/72/77 sts (33/36/38 sts on each side plus 1/0/1 st from shoulder seam).

Row 1 (wrong side): Knit 1, Purl 65/70/75, Knit 1.

Block Pattern—

Sizes 36-38 & 44-46—

Row 1: Knit 1, Purl 5, *Knit 5, Purl 5*. Rep *—* 5/6 more times. Knit 1.

Size 40-42—

Row 1: Knit 1, Purl 5, *Knit 5, Purl 5*. Rep *—* 5 more times. Knit 6.

Sizes 36-38 & 40-42 & 44-46—

Note: Starting on fourth Block, Dec 1 st on each edge every 2 in. (5 cm). Rep 7 times, or until 53/58/63 sts remain.

Continue working Block Pattern until sleeve length is 16/17½/19 in. (40.5/44.5/48 cm), or work to desired length.

Row 7 or 15 (right side): Knit across.

Row 8 or 16: Purl and Dec 15/16/16 sts evenly across.

Cuffs: Change to size 8 needles and work Double Rib for 3½ in. (9 cm). From right side, Bind Off in Ribbing.

BLOCKING & PRESSING:
See pg. 120.

SEAM JOININGS: See pg. 121.

NECKBAND: From right side, Pick Up 72/76/78 sts around neckline. Place on circular needle. Work Single Rib for 1½ in. (4 cm). From right side, Bind Off in Ribbing.

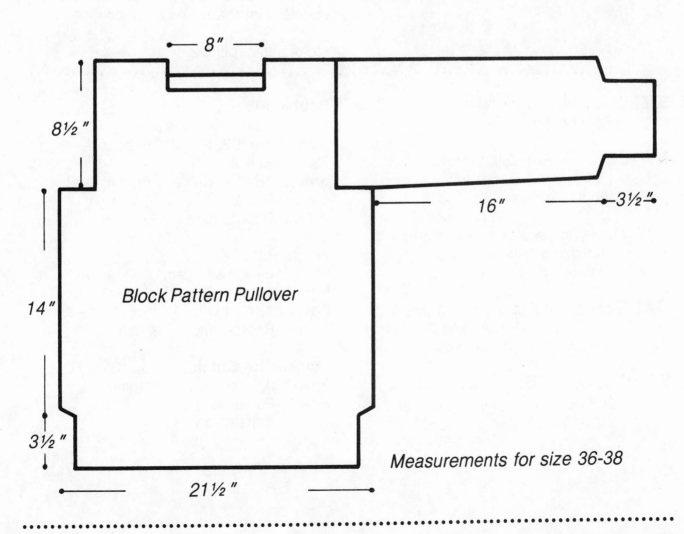

Block Pattern Pullover

Measurements for size 36-38

raspberry pullover

Here's a basic style unique in luscious color, pattern and yarn. Clusters of Knot Stitches are sprinkled along each sleeve, and they also run in vertical panels between rows of Double Rib on the front and back. The pure wool yarn has an unusual bouclé twist that gives extra bounce.

(color photo, page 29)

SIZES: 8-10 / 12-14 / 16-18
For standard sizing, see pg. 11.

MATERIALS: Bois Joli ''Asturias'' (100% wool), imported by Merino Wool. Dk. Rose—14/15/16 skeins @ 1¾ oz. (50 gr) per skein. Knitting needles size 7 (4.5 mm) and size 8 (5 mm). Circular needle size 7 (4.5 mm).

GAUGE: Stockinette Stitch and size 8 needles, 16 stitches and 26 rows = 4 in. (10 cm) square.

STITCHES USED: For abbreviations, see pg. 15. For how to knit, see pg. 108.

Double Rib_____
Worked over 4 stitches plus 2.
Row 1: *Knit 2, Purl 2*. Repeat *—*. Knit 2.
Row 2: *Purl 2, Knit 2*. Repeat *—*. Purl 2.
Repeat rows 1, 2.

Single Rib_____
Worked over 2 stitches.
Row 1: *Knit 1, Purl 1*. Repeat *—*.
Row 2: *Knit 1, Purl 1*. Repeat *—*.
Repeat rows 1, 2.

Stockinette Stitch_____
Row 1 (right side): Knit across.
Row 2: Purl across.
Repeat rows 1, 2.

Knot Stitch Panel

Worked over 11 stitches.

Row 1 (wrong side): *Knit 3, Knit 1/Purl 1/Knit 1/Purl 1/Knit 1 into one stitch*. Repeat *—*. Knit 3.

Row 2: Purl across.

Row 3: *Knit 3, Purl 5 stitches together*. Repeat *—*. Knit 3.

Row 4: Purl across.

Row 5: Knit 5, Knit 1/Purl 1/Knit 1/Purl 1/Knit 1 into one stitch, Knit 5.

Row 6: Purl across.

Row 7: Knit 5, Purl 5 together, Knit 5.

Row 8: Purl across.

Repeat rows 1-8.

Note: Edge stitches are not included in stitch instructions, above. See edge stitches, pg. 116.

BACK: With size 7 needles, Cast On 78/82/94 sts. Work Double Rib for 3 in. (7.5 cm).

Pattern—Change to size 8 needles.

Size 8-10—Inc 7 sts.

Row 1 (right side): Knit 1, Inc 1, Knit 4, Inc 1, Knit 5, Purl 2, *Knit 2, Purl 2, Knit 2, Purl 5, Inc 1, Purl 5*. Rep *—* 2 more times. Knit 2, Purl 2, Knit 2, Purl 2, Knit 5, Inc 1, Knit 4, Inc 1, Knit 1.

Size 12-14—Inc 9 sts.

Row 1 (right side): Knit 1, Inc 1, Knit 3, Inc 1, Knit 4, Inc 1, Knit 4, Purl 2, *Knit 2, Purl 2, Knit 2, Purl 5, Inc 1, Purl 5*. Rep *—* 2 more times. Knit 2, Purl 2, Knit 2, Purl 2, Knit 4, Inc 1, Knit 4, Inc 1, Knit 3, Inc 1, Knit 1.

Size 16-18—Inc 5 sts.

Row 1 (right side): Knit 1, Inc 1, Knit 9, Purl 2, Knit 2, Purl 2, Knit 2, Purl 2, *Knit 2, Purl 2, Knit 2, Purl 5, Inc 1, Purl 5*. Rep *—* 2 more times. *Knit 2, Purl 2*. Rep *—* 3 more times. Knit 9, Inc 1, Knit 1.

Sizes 8-10 & 12-14—85/91 sts.

Row 2: Knit 1 (edge st), Purl 11/14, Knit 2, *Purl 2, Knit 2, Purl 2, Knit 11*. Rep *—* 2 more times. Purl 2, Knit 2, Purl 2, Knit 2, Purl 11/14, Knit 1 (edge st).

Row 3: Knit 12/15, Purl 2, *Knit 2, Purl 2, Knit 2, Purl 11*. Rep *—* 2 more times. Knit 2, Purl 2, Knit 2, Purl 2, Knit 12/15.

Size 16-18—99 sts.

Row 2: Knit 1 (edge st), Purl 10, Knit 2, Purl 2, Knit 2, Purl 2, Knit 2, *Purl 2, Knit 2, Purl 2, Knit 11*. Rep *—* 2 more times. *Purl 2, Knit 2*. Rep *—* 3 more times. Purl 10, Knit 1 (edge st).

Row 3: Knit 11, Purl 2, Knit 2, Purl 2, Knit 2, Purl 2, *Knit 2, Purl 2, Knit 2, Purl 11*. Rep *—* 2 more times. *Knit 2, Purl 2*. Rep *—* 3 more times. Knit 11.

Sizes 8-10 & 12-14 & 16-18—

Row 4 (wrong side): Rep row 2 as far as first Knot Stitch Panel (20/23/27 sts worked). Work row 1 of Knot Stitch Panel (see stitch instructions). Purl 2, Knit 2, Purl 2. Second panel. Purl 2, Knit 2, Purl 2. Third panel. Rep row 2 for remaining sts. Continue working Double Rib & Stockinette Stitch & rows 1-8 of Knot Stitch Panel for 11 in. (28 cm), or work to desired length.

Armholes (right side): Row 2 of Knot Stitch—Bind Off in Knit 8/7/7 sts. Purl 12/16/20 sts (incl. bind off st). Work pattern 45 sts. Purl 11/15/19, Knit 1. Bind Off remaining 8/7/7 sts.

Rows 3, 4: Continue working pattern.

Row 5: Knit 1, *Knit/Purl/Knit/Purl/Knit into one st, Knit 3*. Rep *—* 5/6/7 more times. Knit 1, Purl 2, Knit 2, Purl 2, Knit 5, Knit/Purl/Knit/Purl/Knit into one st, Knit 5, Purl 2, Knit 2, Purl 2, Knit 1, *Knit/Purl/Knit/Purl/Knit into one st, Knit 3*. Rep *—* 4/5/6 more times. Knit/Purl/Knit/Purl/Knit into one st, Knit 1.

Continue working pattern for 5½/6/6½ in. (14/15.5/16.5 cm).

Neck (right side): Row 4 or row 8 of Knot Stitch—Work pattern for 23/26/29 sts. Bind Off in Purl 23/25/27 sts. Work remaining 23/26/29 sts (incl. bind off st).

Shoulders (both stay on needle, but are worked separately): Work pattern until armhole length is 6½/7/7½ in. (16.5/18/19 cm). Bind Off in Purl on row 4 or 8 of Knot Stitch.

FRONT: Work same as Back as far as armholes, plus 4½/5/5½ in. (11.5/13/14 cm).

Neck: Work same as Back.

Shoulders: Work for 2 in. (5 cm).

SHOULDER JOININGS: See pg. 121.

SLEEVES: From right side and on size 8 needle, Pick Up 61/65/69 sts (30/32/34 sts on each side, plus 1 st from shoulder seam).

Stockinette Stitch—

Row 1 (wrong side): Knit across.

Row 2: Knit 1 (edge st), Purl 59/63/67, Knit 1 (edge st).

Knot Stitch—

Row 1: Knit 2, *Knit/Purl/Knit/Purl/Knit into one st, Knit 3*. Rep *—* 13/14/15 more times. Knit/Purl/Knit/Purl/Knit into one st, Knit 2.

Row 2: Knit 1, Purl 59/63/67, Knit 1.

Row 3: Knit 2, *Purl 5 sts tog, Knit 3*. Rep *—* 13/14/15 more times. Purl 5 tog, Knit 2.

Row 4: Knit 1, Purl 59/63/67, Knit 1.

Row 5: Knit 4, *Knit/Purl/Knit/Purl/Knit into one st, Knit 3*. Rep *—* 12/13/14 more times. Knit/Purl/Knit/Purl/Knit into one st, Knit 4.

Row 6: Knit 1, Purl 59/63/67, Knit 1.

Row 7: Knit 4, *Purl 5 tog, Knit 3*. Rep *—* 12/13/14 more times. Purl 5 tog, Knit 4.

Row 8: Knit 1, Purl 59/63/67, Knit 1.

Continue working rows 1-8 of Knot Stitch until sleeve length is 15/15½/16 in. (38/39.5/40.5 cm), or work to desired length.

Stockinette Stitch—

Row 1: Row 1 or row 5 of Knot Stitch—Knit across.

Row 2: Purl and Dec 27 sts evenly across (34/38/42 sts remain).

Cuffs (wrong side): Change to size 7 needles. Work Double Rib for 3 in. (7.5 cm). From right side, Bind Off in Ribbing.

BLOCKING & PRESSING:
See pg. 120.

SEAM JOININGS: See pg. 121.

NECKBAND: From right side, Pick Up 68/72/76 sts around neckline. Place on circular needle. Work Single Rib for 1 in. (2.5 cm). From right side, Bind Off in Ribbing.

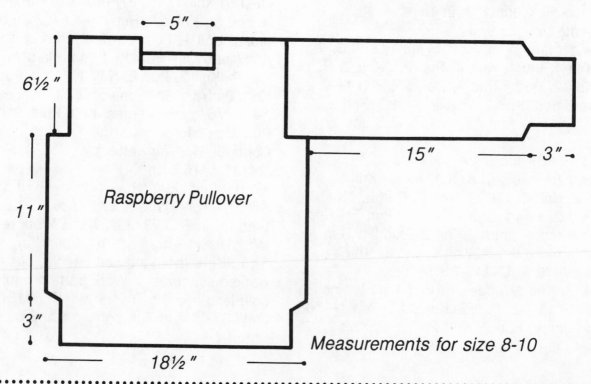

5″

6½″

15″   3″

11″

Raspberry Pullover

3″

18½″

Measurements for size 8-10

multi-blue basic

This is the simplest sweater of them all. It is knitted in Garter Stitch, with an occasional Purl to form a ridge pattern on the sleeves. The rugged tweed wool gives a unique pebbly texture, but the style is adaptable to other yarns. It's a great choice for the beginner.

(color photo, page 29)

SIZES: 6-8 / 10-12 / 14-16 / 18
For standard sizing, see pg. 11.

MATERIALS: Tahki Imports Ltd. "Donegal Tweed Homespun" (100% wool). Blue—5/5/6/7 skeins @ 3½ oz. (100 gr) per skein.
Knitting needles size 7 (4.5 cm).

GAUGE: Garter Stitch, 16 stitches = 4 in. (10 cm).

STITCHES USED: For abbreviations, see pg. 15. For how to knit, see pg. 108.

Garter Stitch_____
Knit every row.
Note: First Knit row is wrong side.

Ridge Pattern for Sleeves_____
Rows 1, 2: Knit across.
Row 3 (wrong side): Purl across.
Rows 4-6: Knit across.
        Repeat rows 3-6.
Note: Knit first and last stitch on row 3.

BACK: Cast On 69/73/77/85 sts and work Garter Stitch for 12 in. (30.5 cm), or work to desired length.
Armholes: From wrong side, Bind Off in Knit 12 sts. Knit 45/49/53/61 sts (incl. bind off st). Bind Off remaining 12 sts. Cut yarn. Attach yarn and start next row. Continue working for 5½/6/6½/7 in. (14/15/16.5/18 cm).
Neck (wrong side): Knit 11/12/13/16. Bind Off in Knit 23/25/27/29 sts. Knit remaining 11/12/13/16 sts (incl. bind off st).
Shoulders (both stay on needle, but are worked separately): Knit 3 more rows. From wrong side, Bind Off in Knit.

FRONT: Work same as Back as far as armholes.

Armholes: From wrong side, Bind Off in Knit 12 sts. Knit 22/24/26/30 (incl. bind off st). Bind Off 1 st in center. Knit 22/24/26/30 (incl. bind off st). Bind Off remaining 12 sts. Cut yarn. Attach yarn and start next row.

Note: Work each side separately (by placing left side on a separate needle), or work both sides together by using a second skein of yarn (attach at left Front opening). Continue working for 4/4½/5/5½ in. (10/11.5/13/14 cm).

Note: Make sure that center edge stitches are worked firmly.

Neck (wrong side): **Right Front**—Knit 11/12/13/16. Bind Off in Knit 11/12/13/14 sts. Cut yarn. Attach yarn as before.

Left Front—Bind Off in Knit 11/12/13/14 sts. Knit remaining 11/12/13/16 sts (incl. bind off st).

Shoulders (worked separately): Work Knit rows for 2 in. (5 cm), or work to match Back armhole length. From wrong side, Bind Off in Knit.

SHOULDER JOININGS: See pg. 121.

SLEEVES: From right side, Pick Up 48/52/56/60 sts (24/26/28/30 sts on each side of shoulder seam).
Follow Ridge Pattern instructions and work 31/32/33/33 repeats. End with row 3. Work Garter Stitch 2½ in. (6.5 cm), or until sleeve length is 17/17½/18/18 in. (43/44.5/45.5/45.5 cm). From wrong side, Bind Off in Knit.

BLOCKING & PRESSING:
See pg. 120.

SEAM JOININGS: See pg. 121.

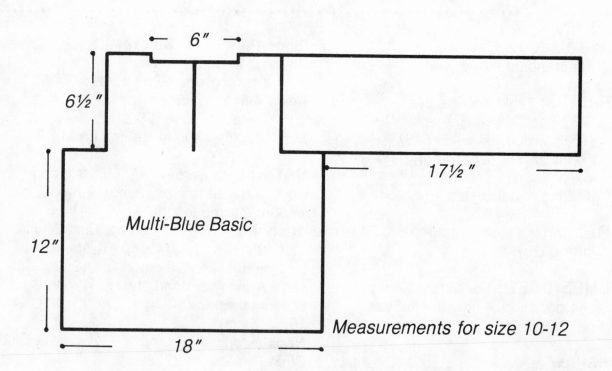

6"

6½"

17½"

12"

Multi-Blue Basic

18"

Measurements for size 10-12

Raspberry Pullover, page 24

Multi-Blue Basic, page 27

29

30　*Block Pattern Pullover, page 21*　　*Lollipop Pullover, page 42*

Fisherman's Knit, page 18   *Rickrack Rib Pullover, page 44*   31

eyelet pullover

This delicate pattern is created by simply alternating a row of Eyelet Stitch with rows of Stockinette. The fullness of the blouson shape is echoed in the full sleeves with gathered cuffs. The multi-shades in the bouclé wool-blend yarn give the sweater a heathery effect.

SIZES: 8-10 / 12-14 / 16-18
For standard sizing, see pg. 11.

MATERIALS: Georges Picaud "Bouclé Sage Chiné" (43% acrylic, 34% wool, 23% kid mohair), imported by Merino Wool. Green-Blue-Pink (multicolor yarn)—7/7/8 skeins @ 1¾ oz. (50 gr) per skein. Knitting needles size 6 (4 mm) and size 7 (4.5 mm). Crochet hook size E (3.5 mm).

GAUGE: Stockinette Stitch and size 7 needles, 16 stitches = 4 in. (10 cm).

STITCHES USED: For abbreviations, see pg. 15. For how to knit, see pg. 108.

Stockinette Stitch
Row 1 (right side): Knit across.
Row 2: Purl across.
   Repeat rows 1, 2.

Eyelet Pattern
Worked over 2 stitches.
Row 1: *Purl 2 together, Yo*. Repeat *—*.
Row 2 (right side): Knit across.
Row 3: Purl across.
   Repeat rows 2, 3, plus row 2.
   Repeat rows 1-6.

Note: Edge stitches are not included in stitch instructions at left. See edge stitches, pg. 116.

BACK: With size 6 needles, Cast On 64/72/80 sts.
Stockinette Stitch—
Row 1 (right side): Knit across.
Row 2: Knit 1 (edge st), Purl 62/70/78, Knit 1 (edge st).
Rep rows 1, 2 two more times.
Row 7: Change to size 7 needles—Knit across and Inc 8 sts. Inc 1 st inside each side edge, remaining 6 sts evenly across.
Eyelet Pattern—
Row 1 (wrong side): Knit 1, *Purl 2 tog, Yo*. Rep *—* 34/38/42 more times. Knit 1.
Row 2: Knit across.
Row 3: Knit 1, Purl, Knit 1.
Rep rows 2, 3, plus row 2.
Continue working rows 1-6 for 13 in. (33 cm), or work to desired length.
Armholes (wrong side): **Row 1**—Bind Off in Purl 10 sts. Work pattern 51/59/67 sts (incl. bind off st). Knit 1. Bind Off remaining 10 sts.
Continue working pattern rows 1-6 for 6/6½/7 in. (15/16.5/18 cm).
Neck: Work pattern 14/16/18 sts. Bind Off in Knit or Purl 24/28/32 sts. Bind Off remaining 14/16/18 sts (incl. bind off st).
Shoulders (both stay on needle, but are worked separately): Work pattern for ½ in. (1.3 cm), or until armhole length is 6½/7/7½ in. (16.5/18/19 cm). Bind Off in Knit or Purl.

FRONT: Work same as Back as far as armhole, plus 3/3½/4 in. (7.5/9/10 cm).
Neck: Work same as Back.
Work each side separately by placing left side on a safety pin.

Continue working pattern until armhole length is 6½/7/7½ in. (16.5/18/19 cm), or work to match Back.

Shoulder: Bind Off in Knit or Purl.

Left side: Work same as right side.

SHOULDER JOININGS: See pg. 121.

SLEEVES: From right side and on size 7 needle, Pick Up 66/70/74 sts (33/35/37 sts on each side of shoulder seam).

Row 1 (wrong side): Knit 1 (edge st), Purl 64/68/72, Knit 1 (edge st).

Row 2: Knit across.

Eyelet Pattern—

Row 1 (wrong side): Knit 1, *Purl 2 tog, Yo*. Rep *—* 31/33/35 more times. Knit 1.

Continue working pattern rows 1-6 until sleeve length is 19/19¾/20½ in. (48.5/50/52 cm), or work to desired length.

Cuffs: Change to size 6 needles—Purl 2 tog across.

Row 1 (right side): Knit across.

Row 2: Purl across.

Rep rows 1, 2 for 1½ in. (4 cm). From right side, Bind Off in Knit.

BLOCKING & PRESSING:
See pg. 120.

SEAM JOININGS: See pg. 121.

NECK FINISHING: Reversed Single Crochet. See pg. 123.

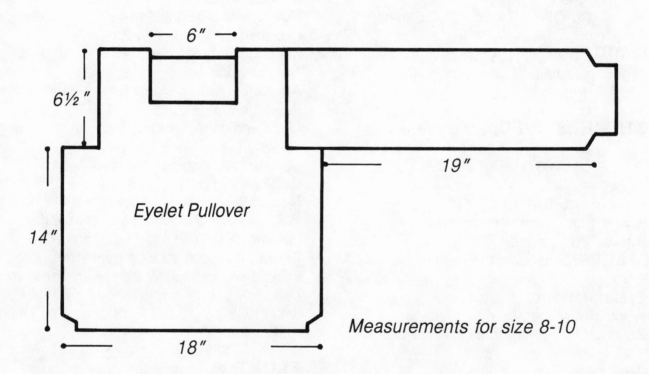

Eyelet Pullover

6"

6½"

14"

18"

19"

Measurements for size 8-10

red lace top

Overlapping leaves gracefully curve upward, creating a romantic lace. This seemingly complicated pattern and the unusually thin, cotton-like acrylic yarn work up with incredible ease and speed.

(color photo, page 49)

SIZES: 6-10 / 12-14
   For standard sizing, see pg. 11.

MATERIALS: Coats & Clark ''Luster-Sheen'' (100% acrylic). Wine Red—5/6 skeins @ 2 oz. (56.7 gr) per skein.
   Knitting needles size 4 (3.5 mm).
   Crochet hook size D (3 mm).

GAUGE: Stockinette Stitch, 18 stitches and 24 rows = 3 in. (7.5 cm) square.

STITCHES USED: For abbreviations, see pg. 15. For how to knit, see pg. 108.

Double Rib

Worked over 4 stitches plus 2.
Row 1: *Knit 2, Purl 2*. Repeat *—*. Knit 2.
Row 2: *Purl 2, Knit 2*. Repeat *—*. Purl 2.
   Repeat rows 1, 2.

Lace Stitch

Worked over 14 stitches plus 1.
Row 1 (right side): Yo, Knit 5, Twist Knit 2 together, Knit 2 together, Knit 5, Yo, Knit 1.
Row 2: Purl across.
Row 3: Knit 1, Yo, Knit 4, Twist Knit 2 tog, Knit 2 tog, Knit 4, Yo, Knit 2.
Row 4: Purl across.
Row 5: Knit 2, Yo, Knit 3, Twist Knit 2 tog, Knit 2 tog, Knit 3, Yo, Knit 3.
Row 6: Purl across.   ▷

Row 7: Knit 3, Yo, Knit 2, Twist Knit 2 tog, Knit 2 tog, Knit 2, Yo, Knit 4.
Row 8: Purl across.
Row 9: Knit 4, Yo, Knit 1, Twist Knit 2 tog, Knit 2 tog, Knit 1, Yo, Knit 5.
Row 10: Purl across.
Row 11: Knit 5, Yo, Twist Knit 2 tog, Knit 2 tog, Yo, Knit 6.
Row 12: Purl across.
Row 13: Knit across.
Row 14: Purl across.
Repeat rows 1-14.

Note: Edge stitches are not included in stitch instructions, above. See edge stitches, pg. 116.

BACK:
Cast On 98/106 sts and work Double Rib for 3 in. (7.5 cm).

Stockinette Stitch—
Row 1 (right side): Knit across and Inc 8/10 sts. Inc 1 st on each edge, remaining 6/8 sts evenly across (106/116 sts).
Row 2: Knit 1 (edge st), Purl 104/114, Knit 1 (edge st).

Lace Stitch Pattern—
Row 1 (right side): Knit 1/3, *Yo, Knit 5, Twist Knit 2 tog, Knit 2 tog, Knit 5, Yo, Knit 1/2*. Rep *—* 6 more times. Knit 0/1.
Row 2: Knit 1, Purl 104/114, Knit 1.
Row 3: Knit 2/4, *Yo, Knit 4, Twist Knit 2 tog, Knit 2 tog, Knit 4, Yo, Knit 3/4*. Rep *—* 5 more times. Yo, Knit 4, Twist Knit 2 tog, Knit 2 tog, Knit 4, Yo, Knit 2/4.
Row 4: Knit 1, Purl 104/114, Knit 1.
Row 5: Knit 3/5, *Yo, Knit 3, Twist Knit 2 tog, Knit 2 tog, Knit 3, Yo, Knit 5/6*. Rep *—* 5 more times. Yo, Knit 3, Twist Knit 2 tog, Knit 2 tog, Knit 3, Yo, Knit 3/5.
Row 6: Knit 1, Purl 104/114, Knit 1.
Row 7: Knit 4/6, *Yo, Knit 2, Twist Knit 2 tog, Knit 2 tog, Knit 2, Yo, Knit 7/8*. Rep *—* 5 more times. Yo, Knit 2, Twist Knit 2 tog, Knit 2 tog, Knit 2, Yo, Knit 4/6.
Row 8: Knit 1, Purl 104/114, Knit 1.
Row 9: Knit 5/7, *Yo, Knit 1, Twist Knit 2 tog, Knit 2 tog, Knit 1, Yo, Knit 9/10*. Rep *—* 5 more times. Yo, Knit 1, Twist Knit 2 tog, Knit 2 tog, Knit 1, Yo, Knit 5/7.
Row 10: Knit 1, Purl 104/114, Knit 1.
Row 11: Knit 6/8, *Yo, Twist Knit 2 tog, Knit 2 tog, Yo, Knit 11/12*. Rep *—* 5 more times. Yo, Twist Knit 2 tog, Knit 2 tog, Yo, Knit 6/8.
Row 12: Knit 1, Purl 104/114, Knit 1.
Row 13: Knit across.
Row 14: Knit 1, Purl 104/114, Knit 1.
Rep rows 1-14 five more times, plus rows 1-12.

Armholes (right side): **Row 13**—Bind Off in Chain Knit 15/17 sts. Work Knit and Bind Off last 15/17 sts. Cut yarn. Attach yarn and start next row.
Row 14: Knit 1, Purl 74/80, Knit 1.
Work pattern rows 1-14 one more time (5 Lace Stitch panels remain).
Row 1: Knit 15/17, *Yo, Knit 5, Twist Knit 2 tog, Knit 2 tog, Knit 5, Yo, Knit 1/2*. Rep *—* 2 more times. Knit 14/15 (3 Lace Stitch panels remain).
Row 2: Knit 1, Purl 74/80, Knit 1.
Continue working pattern rows 1-14 two times, plus rows 1-12.

Neck & Shoulders (right side): **Size 6-10** and row 13—Bind Off in Chain Knit.
Size 12-14—Work rows 13, 14, plus 1 row of Knit, 1 row of Purl. Bind Off in Chain Knit on Knit row (17th row).

FRONT:
Work same as Back as far as 5 Lace Stitch panels, plus rows 1-12 of 3 Lace Stitch panels.

Neck: Knit 16/18. Bind Off in Chain Knit 44/46 sts. Knit remaining 16/18 sts (incl. bind off st).
Work each side separately by placing left side on a safety pin.
Row 1 (wrong side): Knit 1, Purl 14/16, Knit 1.
Row 2: Knit across.
Rep rows 1, 2 for 3/3½ in. (7.5/9 cm).
Shoulder: From right side, Bind Off in Chain Knit.
Left side: Work same as right side.

SHOULDER JOININGS: See pg. 121.

SLEEVES: From right side, Pick Up 79/86 sts (39/43 sts on each side, plus 1/0 st from shoulder seam).
Row 1 (wrong side): Knit 1 (edge st), Purl 77/84, Knit 1 (edge st).
Row 2: Knit across.
Rep rows 1, 2 for 1½ in. (4 cm).
Lace Stitch Pattern—
Row 1 (right side): Knit 10/12, *Yo, Knit 5, Twist Knit 2 tog, Knit 2 tog, Knit 5, Yo, Knit 1/2*. Rep *—* 3 more times. Knit 9/10.
Row 2: Knit 1, Purl 77/84, Knit 1.

Continue working pattern rows 1-14 four times, plus rows 1-12. Or work to desired length.
Row 13 (right side): Knit and Dec 12 sts evenly across.
Row 14: Knit 1, Purl 65/72, Knit 1.
Row 15: Bind Off in Chain Knit.

BLOCKING & PRESSING:
See pg. 120.

SEAM JOININGS: See pg. 121.

NECK & SLEEVE FINISHING:
Reversed Single Crochet. See pg. 123.

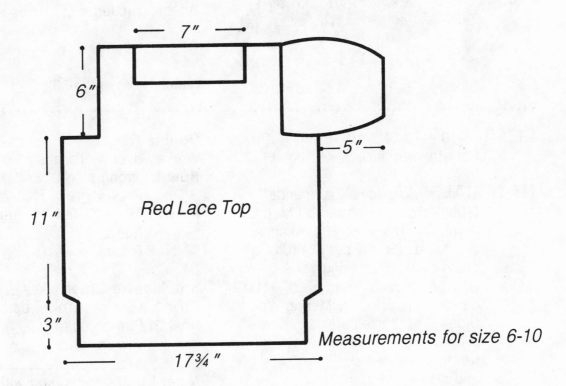

Red Lace Top

Measurements for size 6-10

navy blouson

Here comes navy, billowing in two tones and two yarns. Dark stripes of wool alternate with lighter ridges of wool and cotton to create a subtle, velvety effect. An interesting rolled edge binds the boat neck.

(color photo, page 50)

SIZES: 8-10 / 12-14 / 16-18
For standard sizing, see pg. 11.

MATERIALS: Bois Joli "Clairelande" (100% wool), imported by Merino Wool. Dk. Blue—8/9/10 skeins @ 1¾ oz. (50 gr) per skein, or any chain-twisted fingering yarn. Georges Picaud "Fric Frac" (100% cotton), imported by Merino Wool. Blue—5/6/7 skeins @ 1²/₅ oz. (40 gr) per skein.
Knitting needles size 4 (3.5 mm) and size 7 (4.5 mm).
Circular needle size 4 (3.5 mm).

GAUGE: Stockinette Stitch with 2 strands and size 7 needles, 20 stitches = 4 in. (10 cm).

STITCHES USED: For abbreviations, see pg. 15. For how to knit, see pg. 108.

Double Rib
Worked over 4 stitches plus 2.
Row 1 (wrong side): *Knit 2, Purl 2*. Repeat *—*. Knit 2.
Row 2: *Purl 2, Knit 2*. Repeat *—*. Purl 2.
Repeat rows 1, 2.

Stockinette Stitch
Row 1 (right side): Knit across.
Row 2: Purl across.
Repeat rows 1, 2.

Note: Dk. Blue—worked with 2 strands of wool.

Garter Stitch
Knit every row.

Note: Mixed Blue—worked with 1 strand of wool and 1 strand of cotton.

BACK: With Dk. Blue and size 4 needles, Cast On 78/90/98 sts and work Double Rib for 2½ in. (6.5 cm).
Row 1 (right side): Change to size 7 needles. Knit across and Inc 14/12/12 sts. Inc 1 st on each side edge, remaining 12/10/10 sts evenly across.
Row 2: Purl across.
Rows 3, 4: Work Stockinette Stitch.
Ridge Pattern—
Rows 1, 2: Mixed Blue—Knit across.
Rows 3, 4: Dk. Blue—Work Stockinette Stitch.
Rep rows 1-4 twenty-two (22) more times, plus rows 1-3. Ridge Pattern measures 12 in. (30.5 cm). Or work to desired length.
Armholes (wrong side): **Row 4**—Bind Off in Purl 12/14/16 sts. Purl 68/74/78 (incl. bind off st). Bind Off remaining 12/14/16 sts. Cut yarns. Attach yarns and start next row.
Continue working rows 1-4 for 10/11/12 times, plus row 1.
Neck (wrong side): **Row 2**—Knit 12/14/16. Bind Off in Knit 44/46/46 sts. Knit remaining 12/14/16 sts (incl. bind off st).
Shoulders (both stay on needle, but are worked separately): Work rows 3, 4 plus rows 1-4, plus row 1. Armhole length is 6½/7/7½ in. (16.5/18/19 cm). From wrong side, Bind Off in Knit.

FRONT: Work same as Back.

SHOULDER JOININGS: See pg. 121.

SLEEVES: With Mixed Blue and size 7 needle, from right side, Pick Up 66/68/70 sts (33/34/35 sts on each side of shoulder seam).
Continue to work Ridge Pattern until sleeve length is 16/16½/17 in. (40.5/42/43 cm), or work to desired length. End on pattern row 3.
Row 4: Purl and Dec 28/26/24 sts evenly across.
Cuffs: Change to size 4 needles. Work Double Rib for 2½ in. (6.5 cm). From right side, Bind Off in Ribbing.

BLOCKING & PRESSING: See pg. 120.

SEAM JOININGS: See pg. 121.

NECKBAND: With Mixed Blue, from right side, Pick Up 108/112/112 sts. Place on circular needle.
Row 1 (wrong side): Knit 1 round.
Row 2: Knit 1 round.
Row 3: Purl 1 round.
Rep rows 2, 3 three more times. From right side, Bind Off in Knit.

NECK FINISHING (wrong side): Fold neckband in half and attach bind off edge to inside of neckline.

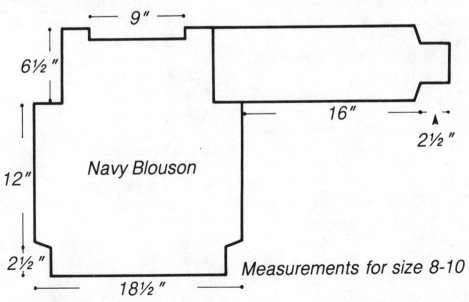

9"
6½"
16"
2½"
12"
2½"
18½"
Navy Blouson
Measurements for size 8-10

fluffy mohair

This soft, bulky sweater in a wool-and-mohair-blend yarn is wonderfully warm for wearing outdoors. A Stockinette Stitch in solid blue creates a yoke effect at the top, while rows in taupe and white stripe the body and sleeves.

(color photo, page 50)

SIZES: 8-10 / 12-14 / 16-18
For standard sizing, see pg. 11.

MATERIALS: Pingouin ''Laine et Mohair'' (70% wool, 25% mohair, 5% polyamide). Dk. Blue—3/3/4 skeins; Ecru and Taupe—4/4/5 skeins each @ 1¾ oz. (50 gr) per skein.
Knitting needles size 7 (4.5 mm) and size 8 (5 mm).
Crochet hook size F (4 mm).

GAUGE: Stockinette Stitch, 16 stitches and 20 rows = 4 in. (10 cm) square.

STITCHES USED: For abbreviations, see pg. 15. For how to knit, see pg. 108.

Double Rib_____
Worked over 4 stitches plus 2.

Row 1: *Knit 2, Purl 2*. Repeat *—*. Knit 2.
Row 2: *Purl 2, Knit 2*. Repeat *—*. Purl 2.
Repeat rows 1, 2.

Stockinette Stitch_____
Row 1 (right side): Knit across.
Row 2: Purl across.
Repeat rows 1, 2.

Garter Stitch_____
Knit every row.

BACK: With Dk. Blue and size 7 needles, Cast On 78/86/94 sts. Work Double Rib for 3 in. (7.5 cm).
Stockinette & Garter Stitch—Change to size 8 needles.
Row 1 (right side): Knit across.
Row 2: Purl across.
Rep rows 1, 2.
Rows 5, 6: Ecru—Knit across.

Row 7 (right side): Taupe—Knit across.
Row 8: Purl across.
Rows 9, 10: Ecru—Knit across.
Row 11 (right side): Taupe—Knit across.
Row 12: Purl across.
Rows 13, 14: Ecru—Knit across.
Rep rows 1-14 four more times, or work to desired length.
Stockinette Stitch—
Row 1 (right side): Dk. Blue—Knit across.
Row 2: Purl across.
Row 3: Knit across.
Armholes (wrong side): Bind Off in Purl 12 sts. Purl across and Bind Off last 12 sts. Continue working Stockinette Stitch for 5/5½/6 in. (12.5/14/15 cm).
Neck (wrong side): Purl 14/16/18. Bind Off in Purl 26/30/34 sts. Purl remaining 14/16/18 sts (incl. bind off st).
Shoulders (both stay on needle, but are worked separately): Work for 1½ in. (4 cm). From wrong side, Bind Off in Purl.

FRONT: Work same as Back.

SHOULDER JOININGS: See pg. 121.

SLEEVES: With Ecru and size 8 needle,

from right side, Pick Up 52/56/60 sts (26/28/30 sts on each side of shoulder seam).
Row 1 (wrong side): Knit across.
Stockinette & Garter Stitch—
Row 1 (right side): Taupe—Knit across.
Row 2: Purl across.
Rows 3, 4: Ecru—Knit across.
Rep rows 1-4 for 22/23/24 more times.
Stockinette Stitch—
Row 1 (right side): Dk. Blue—Knit across.
Row 2: Purl across.
Rep rows 1, 2.
Cuffs: Change to size 7 needles. Work Double Rib for 3 in. (7.5 cm), or work to desired length. From right side, Bind Off in Ribbing.

BLOCKING & PRESSING:
See pg. 120.

SEAM JOININGS: See pg. 121.

NECK FINISHING: Reversed Single Crochet. See pg. 123.

YARN FINISHING: Brush sweater carefully with a medium-hard brush, using short strokes.

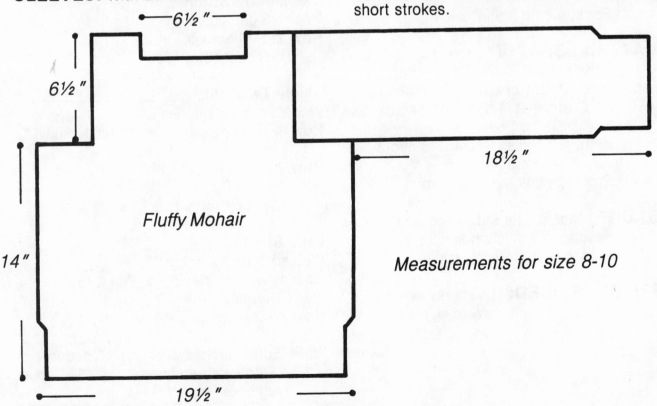

Fluffy Mohair

Measurements for size 8-10

6½"

6½"

18½"

14"

19½"

lollipop pullover

Four happy colors in a fine, gentle wool blend are worked alternately. Each Stockinette Stitch stripe is bordered with a raised line of lace work. Both waist and cuffs are worked in Single Twist Rib.

(color photo, page 30)

SIZES: 4-5 / 6-7 / 8-10
For standard sizing, see pg. 11.

MATERIALS: Phildar ''Pronostic'' (80% acrylic, 20% wool). Orange and Dk. Pink—2/2/1 skeins each; Pink and Lt. Orange—1/1/2 skeins each @ 1¾ oz. (50 gr) per skein.
Knitting needles size 4 (3.5 mm) and size 6 (4 mm).
Crochet hook size E (3.5 mm).

GAUGE: Stockinette Stitch and size 6 needles, 18 stitches and 28 rows = 4 in. (10 cm) square.

STITCHES USED: For abbreviations, see pg. 15. For how to knit, see pg. 108.

Stockinette Stitch_____
Row 1 (right side): Knit across.
Row 2: Purl across.
    Repeat rows 1, 2.

Single Twist Rib_____
Worked over 2 stitches plus 1.
Row 1 (wrong side): *Twist Knit 1, Purl 1*. Repeat *—*. Twist Knit 1.
Row 2: *Purl 1, Twist Knit 1*. Repeat *—*. Purl 1.
    Repeat rows 1, 2.

Lace Stitch_____
Worked over 2 stitches.
Row 1 (wrong side): *Yo, Purl 2 together*. Repeat *—*.
Row 2: Change color—Knit across.
_____
Note: Edge stitches are not included in stitch instructions, above. See edge stitches, pg. 116.

BACK: With Dk. Pink and size 4 needles, Cast On 57/61/65 sts. Work Single Twist Rib for 2½ in. (6.5 cm).
Stockinette Stitch—Change to size 6 needles.
Row 1 (right side): Knit across and Inc 5 sts. Inc 1 st on each edge, remaining 3 sts evenly across.
Row 2: Knit 1 (edge st), Purl 60/64/68, Knit 1 (edge st).
Row 3: Knit across.
Rep rows 2, 3.
Lace Stitch—
Row 6 (wrong side): Knit 1, *Yo, Purl 2 tog*. Rep *—* 29/31/33 more times. Knit 1.
Orange—
Rows 1, 3, 5: Knit across.
Rows 2, 4: Knit 1, Purl 60/64/68, Knit 1.
Row 6: Knit 1, *Yo, Purl 2 tog*. Rep *—* 29/31/33 more times. Knit 1.
Lt. Orange—Rep rows 1-6.
Pink—Rep rows 1-6.
Orange—Rep rows 1-6.
Lt. Orange—Rep rows 1-6.
Dk. Pink—Rep rows 1-6.
Orange—Rep rows 1-6.
Lt. Orange—Rep rows 1-6.
Pink—Rep rows 1-6.
Orange—Rep rows 1-5.
Add stripes for extra length following stripe repeat.
Armholes (wrong side): **Row 6**—Bind Off in Purl 9 sts. Work pattern 44/48/52 sts (incl. bind off st). Bind Off remaining 9 sts. Cut yarn. Attach yarn and start next row. Continue to work 5 more stripes.
Neck (wrong side): Work 10/12/12 sts. Bind Off in Chain Knit 24/24/28 sts. Work remaining 10/12/12 sts (incl. bind off st).
Shoulders (both stay on needle, but are worked separately): Work last stripe (Orange) until armhole length is 4½/5/5½ in. (11.5/13/14 cm). Bind Off in Chain Knit.

FRONT: Work same as Back.

SHOULDER JOININGS: See pg. 121.

SLEEVES (right side): With Orange and size 6 needle, Pick Up 48/52/56 sts (24/26/28 sts on each side of shoulder seam).
Stockinette Stitch—
Row 1 (wrong side): Knit 1 (edge st), Purl 46/50/54, Knit 1 (edge st).
Row 2: Knit across.
Lace Stitch—
Row 3: Knit 1, *Yo, Purl 2 tog*. Rep *—* 23/24/26 more times. Knit 1.
Lt. Orange—Rep rows 1-6.
Continue working stripes until sleeve length is 9/10/11½ in. (23/25.5/29 cm), or work to desired length (always complete stripe).
Row 1 (wrong side): Purl and Dec 9/11/13 sts evenly across.
Cuffs: Change to size 4 needles. Work Single Twist Rib for 4 in. (10 cm). From wrong side, Bind Off in Ribbing.

BLOCKING & PRESSING: See pg. 120.

SEAM JOININGS: See pg. 121.

NECK FINISHING: Reversed Single Crochet in Dk. Pink. See pg. 123.

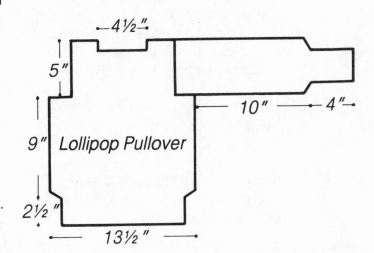

Measurements for size 6-7

rickrack rib pullover

A sweater in super-soft Shetland wool gets extra warmth from an unusual allover Open Rickrack Stitch. Regular Double Rib forms the turtleneck, cuffs and waist. The ''bleached'' denim blue color gives a rugged look.

(color photo, page 31)

SIZES: 4-5 / 6-7 / 8-10
For standard sizing, see pg. 11.

MATERIALS: Aarlan ''Shetland'' (100% wool), imported by Merino Wool.
Lt. Blue—6/7/7 skeins @ 1¾ oz. (50 gr) per skein.
Knitting needles size 4 (3.5 mm) and size 8 (5 mm).
Circular needle size 4 (3.5 mm).

GAUGE: Open Rickrack Stitch and size 8 needles, 24 stitches = 4 in. (10 cm).

STITCHES USED: For abbreviations, see pg. 15. For how to knit, see pg. 108.

Double Rib_____
Worked over 4 stitches plus 2.

Row 1: *Knit 2, Purl 2*. Repeat *—*. Knit 2.
Row 2: *Purl 2, Knit 2*. Repeat *—*. Purl 2.
Repeat rows 1, 2.

Open Rickrack_____
Worked over 2 stitches.
Row 1 (right side): *Pass right-hand needle behind first stitch, Twist Knit second stitch, Knit first stitch, drop both stitches from left-hand needle*. Repeat *—*.
Row 2: *Pass right-hand needle in front of first stitch, Purl second stitch, Purl first stitch, drop both stitches from left-hand needle*. Repeat *—*.
Repeat rows 1, 2.

_____
Note: Edge stitches are not included in stitch instructions, above. See edge stitches, pg. 116.

BACK: With size 4 needles, Cast On 74/82/90 sts and work Double Rib for 2½ in. (6.5 cm).
Stockinette Stitch—Change to size 8 needles.
Row 1 (right side): Knit across and Inc 6/4/4 sts. Inc 1 on each edge, remaining 4/2/2 sts evenly across.
Row 2: Knit 1 (edge st), Purl 78/84/92, Knit 1 (edge st).
Open Rickrack Stitch—
Row 1: Knit 1, *pass right-hand needle behind first st, Twist Knit second st, Knit first st, drop both sts*. Rep *—* 38/41/45 more times. Knit 1.
Row 2: Knit 1, pass right-hand needle in front of first st, Purl second st, Purl first st, drop both sts*. Rep *—* 38/41/45 more times. Knit 1..
Rep rows 1, 2 for 8 in. (20.5 cm), or work to desired length.
Armholes (right side): Bind Off in Knit 10 sts. Work pattern 60/66/74 sts (incl. bind off st). Bind Off remaining 10 sts. Cut yarn. Attach yarn and start next row. Continue working for 3½/4/4½ in. (9/10/11.5 cm).
Neck (right side): Work pattern 18/20/23 sts. Bind Off in Knit 24/26/28 sts. Work remaining 18/20/23 sts (incl. bind off st).
Shoulders (both stay on needle, but are worked separately): Work pattern for 1 in. (2.5 cm). From right side, Bind Off in Knit.

FRONT: Work same as Back.

SHOULDER JOININGS: See pg. 121.

SLEEVES: From right side and on size 8 needle, Pick Up 54/60/66 sts (27/30/33 sts on each side of shoulder seam).
Row 1 (wrong side): Knit 1 (edge st), Purl 52/58/64, Knit 1 (edge st).
Open Rickrack Stitch—
Continue to work pattern rows 1, 2 until sleeve length is 9/10/11½ in. (23/25.5/29 cm), or work to desired length.
Stockinette Stitch—
Row 1 (right side): Knit across.
Row 2: Purl and Dec 18/20/22 sts evenly across.
Cuffs: Change to size 4 needles. Work Double Rib for 4 in. (10 cm). From wrong side, Bind Off in Ribbing.

BLOCKING & PRESSING:
See pg. 120.

SEAM JOININGS: See pg. 121.

TURTLENECK: From right side, Pick Up 76/80/84 sts around neckline. Place on circular needle. Work Double Rib for 5 in. (12.5 cm). From wrong side, Bind Off in Ribbing.

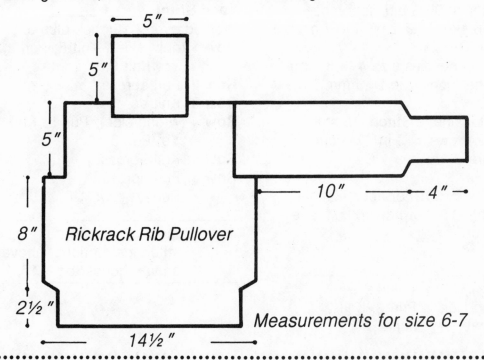

Rickrack Rib Pullover

5"
5"
5"
8"
2½"
14½"
10"
4"

Measurements for size 6-7

jade top

Narrow ribs of lace are worked between wide bands of Stockinette Stitch to create a shadowy rib effect. The fast-knitting acrylic yarn works up like cotton.

(color photo, page 49)

SIZES: 6-10 / 12-14 / 16
For standard sizing, see pg. 11.

MATERIALS: Coats & Clark ''Luster-Sheen'' (100% acrylic). Jade—5/5/6 skeins @ 2 oz. (56.7 gr) per skein.
Knitting needles size 4 (3.5 mm).
Crochet hook size D (3 mm).

GAUGE: Stockinette Stitch, 18 stitches and 24 rows = 3 in. (7.5 cm) square.

STITCHES USED: For abbreviations, see pg. 15. For how to knit, see pg. 108.

Double Rib_____
Worked over 4 stitches plus 2.
Row 1 (wrong side): *Purl 2, Knit 2*.
Repeat *—*. Purl 2.

Row 2: *Knit 2, Purl 2*. Repeat *—*.
Knit 2.
Repeat rows 1, 2.

Lace Stitch_____
Worked over 7 stitches plus 5.
Row 1 (right side): Knit 5, Purl 2 together, Yo, Knit 5.
Row 2: Purl across.
Row 3: Knit across.
Row 4 (wrong side): Purl 5, Knit 2 together, Yo, Purl 5.
Row 5: Knit across.
Row 6: Purl across.
Repeat rows 1-6.

_____
Note: Edge stitches are not included in stitch instructions, above. See edge stitches, pg. 116.

BACK: Cast On 98/110/114 sts and work Double Rib for 3 in. (7.5 cm).
Stockinette Stitch—
Row 1 (right side): Knit across and Inc 9/6/8 sts. Inc 1 st on each side edge, remaining 7/4/6 sts evenly across.
Row 2: Knit 1 (edge st), Purl 105/114/120, Knit 1 (edge st).
Lace Stitch Pattern—
Row 1 (right side): Knit 7/5/8, *Purl 2 tog, Yo, Knit 5/6/6*. Rep *—* 12 more times. Purl 2 tog, Yo, Knit 7/5/8.
Row 2: Knit 1, Purl 105/114/120, Knit 1.
Row 3: Knit across.
Row 4 (wrong side): Knit 1, Purl 6/4/7, *Knit 2 tog, Yo, Purl 5/6/6*. Rep *—* 12 more times. Knit 2 tog, Yo, Purl 6/4/7, Knit 1.
Row 5: Knit across.
Row 6: Knit 1, Purl 105/114/120, Knit 1.
Rep rows 1-6 for 11½ in. (29 cm), or work to desired length. End on row 4.
Armholes (right side): **Row 5**—Bind Off in Chain Knit 18 sts. Knit 71/80/86 (incl. bind off st). Bind Off remaining 18 sts. Cut yarn. Attach yarn and start next row.
Row 6: Knit 1, Purl 69/78/84, Knit 1.
Row 1: Knit 3/3/6, *Purl 2 tog, Yo, Knit 5/6/6*. Rep *—* 8 more times. Knit 3/3/6.
Continue working pattern for 5/5½/6 in. (13/14/15 cm).
Note: Last row worked is pattern row 1 or 4.
Neck Panel: Row 2 or 5—Purl (or Knit) across.
Row 3 or 6: Knit (or Purl) across.
Row 4 or 1: Work pattern for 15/17/20 sts, Purl (or Knit) across 6 Lace Stitch panels. Work pattern for remaining 15/17/20 sts. Continue working Lace Stitch pattern and Knit (or Purl) for 1 or 2 more rows.
Note: End on row 2 or 6.
Neck (right side): **Row 3 or 1**—Knit (or work pattern) 15/17/20 sts. Bind Off in Chain Knit 41/46/46 sts. Knit (or work pattern) remaining 15/17/20 sts (incl. bind off st).

Shoulders (both stay on needle, but are worked separately): Work pattern 5 more rows or until armhole length is 6/6½/7 in. (15/16.5/18 cm). From right side, Bind Off in Chain Knit.

FRONT: Work same as Back as far as armholes, plus 2 in. (5 cm).
Neck Panel: Work same as Back.
Neck: Work same as Back.
Note: Work each side separately by placing Left side on a safety pin.
Work pattern until armhole length is 6/6½/7 in. (15/16.5/18 cm), or work to match Back.
Shoulder: From right side, Bind Off in Chain Knit.
Left side: Work same as right side.

SHOULDER JOININGS: See pg. 121.

SLEEVES: From right side, Pick Up 73/80/86 sts (36/40/43 sts on each side plus 1/0/0 st from shoulder seam).
Row 1 (wrong side): Knit 1 (edge st), Purl 71/78/84, Knit 1 (edge st).
Row 2: Knit 3/3/4, Purl 2 tog, Yo, Knit 13/13/15, *Purl 2 tog, Yo, Knit 3/4/4*. Rep *—* 6 more times. Purl 2 tog, Yo, Knit 13/13/15, Purl 2 tog, Yo, Knit 3/3/4.
Continue working Lace Stitch pattern for 7½ in. (19 cm).
Note: Last row worked is row 1 of Lace Stitch pattern.
Row 2: Knit 1, Purl 71/78/84, Knit 1.
Row 3: Knit across and Dec evenly 10/9/11 sts.
Double Rib—
From wrong side, start working Double Rib, and work for 2 in. (5 cm). From wrong side, Bind Off in Ribbing.

BLOCKING & PRESSING:
See pg. 120.

SEAM JOININGS: See pg. 121.

NECK FINISHING: Reversed Single Crochet. See pg. 123. ▷

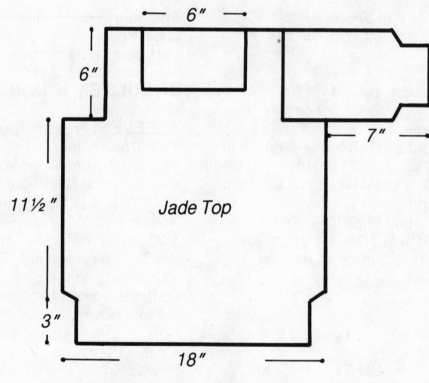

Measurements for size 6-10

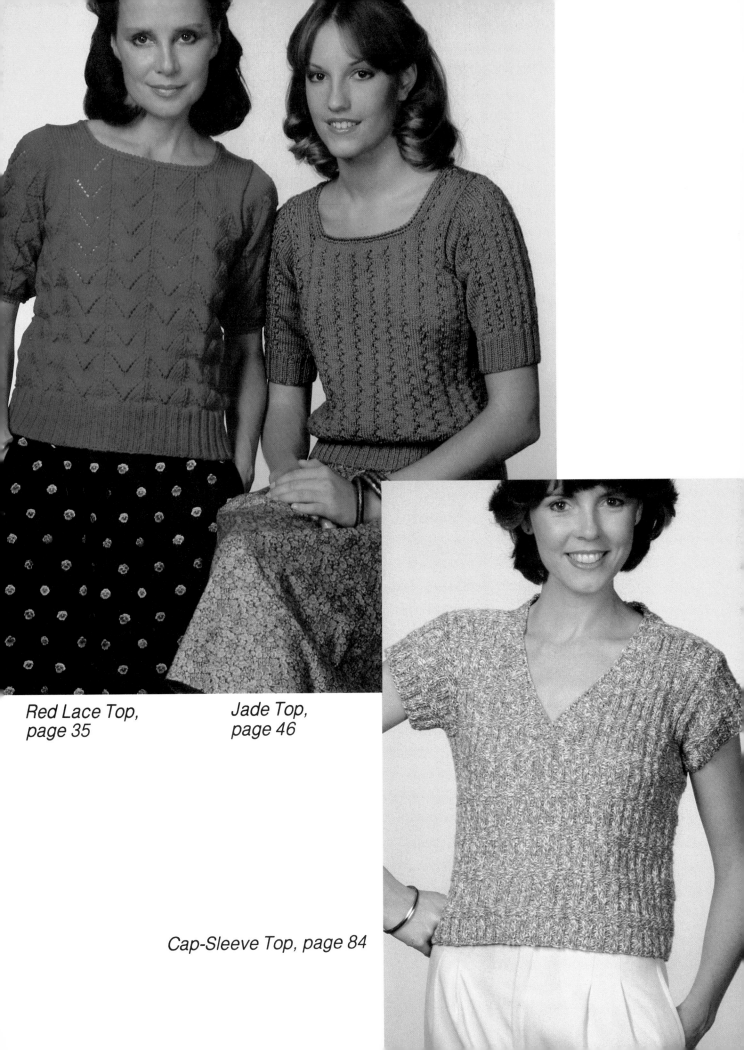

Red Lace Top,
page 35

Jade Top,
page 46

Cap-Sleeve Top, page 84

Fluffy Mohair, page 40

Navy Blouson,
page 38

50

Fair Isle Pullover, page 56

Striped Turtleneck, page 59

fair isle cardigan

This peasanty cardigan, patterned with a simple Fair Isle design and ridged stripes, is worked in multi-textured yarn. The added front-and-neck band is in Single Rib, while waist and cuffs are worked in Double Rib.

SIZES: 6-8 / 10-12 / 14-16
For standard sizing, see pg. 11.

MATERIALS: Phildar "Dundee" (75% acrylic, 15% wool, 10% mohair). Blue—6/7/7 skeins; Red—2/3/3 skeins @ 1¾ oz. (50 gr) per skein.
Phildar "Anouchka" (80% acrylic, 16% mohair, 4% wool). Coral—2/3/3 skeins @ 1²/₅ oz. (40 gr) per skein.
Knitting needles size 6 (4 mm) and size 7 (4.5 mm).
Circular needle size 6 (4 mm).
5 buttons.

GAUGE: Stockinette Stitch and size 7 needles, 18 stitches and 22 rows = 4 in. (10 cm) square.

STITCHES USED: For abbreviations, see pg. 15. For how to knit, see pg. 108.

Double Rib
Worked over 4 stitches plus 2.
Row 1 (wrong side): *Knit 2, Purl 2*. Repeat *—*. Knit 2.
Row 2: *Purl 2, Knit 2*. Repeat *—*. Purl 2.
Repeat rows 1, 2.

Single Rib
Worked over 2 stitches.
Row 1: *Knit 1, Purl 1*. Repeat *—*.
Row 2: *Knit 1, Purl 1*. Repeat *—*.
Repeat rows 1, 2.

Stockinette Stitch
Row 1 (right side): Knit across.
Row 2: Purl across.
Repeat rows 1, 2.

Ridge—Garter Stitch
Row 1 (wrong side): Knit across.
Row 2: Knit across.
Row 3: Change color—Knit across.

Note: Work Coral with 2 strands throughout.
Note: Edge stitches are not included in stitch instructions, above. See edge stitches, pg. 116.

BACK: With Blue and size 6 needles, Cast On 62/70/82 sts. Work Double Rib by alternating 2 rows of Blue and 2 rows of Red for 3 in. (7.5 cm), ending with 2 rows of Blue.
Fair Isle & Stripe Pattern—Change to size 7 needles.
Row 1 (right side): Knit across and Inc 8/10/8 sts. Inc 1 st on each side edge, remaining 6/8/6 sts evenly across.
Row 2: Knit 1 (edge st), Purl 68/78/88, Knit 1 (edge st).
Row 3: Knit across.
Row 4: Knit 1, Purl 68/78/88, Knit 1.
Row 5: *Blue—Knit 1, Coral—Knit 1*. Rep *—* 33/38/43 more times. Blue—Knit 2.
Row 6: Knit 1, Purl 68/78/88, Knit 1.
Row 7: Knit across.
Row 8: Blue—Knit 1, *Coral—Purl 1, Blue—Purl 1*. Rep *—* 32/37/42 more times. Coral—Purl 1, Blue—Purl 1, Knit 1.
Row 9: Knit across.
Row 10: Knit 1, Purl 68/78/88, Knit 1.
Row 11: Knit across.
Row 12: Red—Knit 1, Purl 68/78/88, Knit 1.
Row 13: Knit across.
Row 14 (wrong side): Coral—Knit across.
Row 15: Knit across.

Row 16 (wrong side): Red—Knit across.
Row 17: Knit across.
Row 18: Blue—Knit 1, Purl 68/78/88, Knit 1.
Row 19: Knit across.
Row 20: Red—Knit 1, Purl 68/78/88, Knit 1.
Row 21: Knit across.
Row 22 (wrong side): Coral—Knit across.
Row 23: Knit across.
Row 24 (wrong side): Red—Knit across.
Row 25: Knit across.
Rep rows 2-25, plus rows 2-24.
Armholes (right side): **Row 25**—Bind Off in Knit 6 sts. Work pattern 58/68/78 sts (incl. bind off st). Bind Off remaining 6 sts. Cut yarn. Attach yarn and start next row.
Rep rows 2-8.
Size 6-8—Rep rows 3-8 three more times, plus rows 3-7. Armhole length is 6 in. (15 cm).
Size 10-12—Rep rows 3-8 four more times, plus row 3. Armhole length is 6½ in. (16.5 cm).
Size 14-16—Rep rows 3-8 four more times, plus rows 3-5. Armhole length is 7 in. (18 cm).
Neck & Shoulders (wrong side): Bind Off in Purl 16/19/22 sts. Work 26/30/34 sts (incl. bind off st). Place on safety pin. Bind Off remaining 16/19/22 sts.

RIGHT FRONT: With Blue and size 6 needles, Cast On 30/34/38 sts. Work Double Rib (same as Back).
Fair Isle & Stripe Pattern—Change to size 7 needles.
Row 1 (right side): Knit across and Inc 4/4/6 sts. Inc 1 st on side edge, remaining 3/3/5 sts evenly across.
Row 2: Knit 1 (edge st), Purl 32/36/42, Knit 1 (edge st).
Continue working pattern rows 2-25 twice, plus row 2.
Note: Starting on row 3, Dec 1 st every third row on Front edge until 16/19/22 sts remain.

Continue to work rows 3-24.
Armhole (right side): **Row 25**—Work pattern and Bind Off last 6 sts. Cut yarn. Attach yarn and start next row.
Shoulder (wrong side): Match Back armhole length. Bind Off in Purl 16/19/22 sts.

LEFT FRONT: Work same as right Front, but in reverse.

SHOULDER JOININGS: See pg. 121.

SLEEVES: With Blue and size 7 needle, from right side, Pick Up 54/58/62 sts (27/29/31 sts on each side of shoulder seam).
Row 1: Blue—Knit 1, Purl 52/56/60, Knit 1.
Row 2: Knit across.
Row 3: Red—Knit 1, Purl 52/56/60, Knit 1.
Row 4: Knit across.
Row 5 (wrong side): Coral—Knit across.
Row 6: Knit across.
Row 7 (wrong side): Red—Knit across.
Row 8: Knit across.
Rep rows 1-8 three more times, plus row 1.
Fair Isle Pattern—
Row 1 (right side): Knit across.
Row 2: Knit 1, Purl 52/56/60, Knit 1.
Row 3: *Blue—Knit 1, Coral—Knit 1*. Rep *—* 25/27/29 more times. Blue—Knit 2.
Row 4: Knit 1, Purl 52/56/60, Knit 1.
Row 5: Knit across.
Row 6: Blue—Knit 1, *Coral—Purl 1, Blue—Purl 1*. Rep *—* 24/26/28 more times. Coral—Purl 1, Blue—Purl 1, Knit 1.
Rep rows 1-6 for 8/9/10 more times, plus rows 1-3. Sleeve length is 14½/15/15½ in. (37/38/39.5 cm). Or work to desired length.
Row 4: Purl and Dec 24 sts evenly across.
Cuffs: Change to size 6 needles and work Double Rib (same as Back waist). From wrong side, Bind Off in Ribbing.

BLOCKING & PRESSING:
See pg. 120.

SEAM JOININGS: See pg. 121.

FRONT BAND: With Blue and from right side, Pick Up 198/206/214 sts around entire opening (incl. sts from safety pin). Place on circular needle and work Single Rib as on straight needles for 3 rows.

Buttonholes (right side): **Row 4**—Knit 1, Purl 1, *Bind Off in Knit 2 sts. Work Single Rib for 7 sts*. Rep *—* 4 more times. Continue to work Single Rib.
Row 5: Work Single Rib and Inc 2 sts over every buttonhole.
Work 1 more row. Bind Off in Ribbing.

FINISHING: Attach buttons to left Front band.

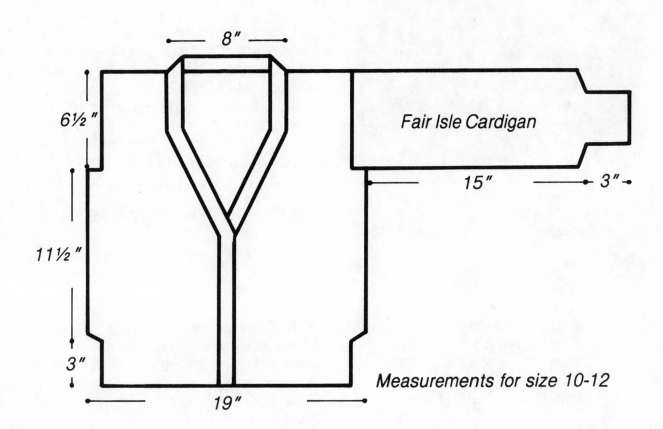

Fair Isle Cardigan

Measurements for size 10-12

8"
6½"
11½"
3"
19"
15"
3"

fair isle pullover

A simple Fair Isle design is worked with double strands of soft wool-blend yarns for extra warmth. Garter Stitch stripes create a dimensional effect. Cables cover the shoulders and add a surprising touch to the waist and cuffs.

(color photo, page 51)

SIZES: 8-10 / 12-14 / 16-18
For standard sizing, see pg. 11.

MATERIALS: Phildar ''Anouchka'' (80% acrylic, 16% mohair, 4% wool). Dk. Blue—10/11/12 skeins; Coral and Red—3/3/4 skeins each @ 1²/₅ oz. (40 gr) per skein. Knitting needles size 6 (4 mm) and size 8 (5 mm). Crochet hook size F (4 mm).

GAUGE: Stockinette Stitch with 2 strands and size 8 needles, 20 stitches and 22 rows = 4 in. (10 cm) square.

STITCHES USED: For abbreviations, see pg. 15. For how to knit, see pg. 108.

Double Rib_____
Worked over 4 stitches plus 2.

Row 1: *Knit 2, Purl 2*. Repeat *—*. Knit 2.
Row 2: *Purl 2, Knit 2*. Repeat *—*. Purl 2.
Repeat rows 1, 2.

Yarn Over Cable_____
Worked over 3 stitches plus 4.
Row 1 (right side): Purl 2, Slip 1, Knit 2, Psso, Purl 2.
Row 2: Knit 2, Purl 1, Yo, Purl 1, Knit 2.
Row 3: Purl 2, Knit 3, Purl 2.
Row 4: Knit 2, Purl 3, Knit 2.
Repeat rows 1-4.
Note: All Slip Stitches are slipped purlwise with yarn in back.

Stockinette Stitch_____
Row 1 (right side): Knit across.
Row 2: Purl across.
Repeat rows 1, 2.

Ridge—Garter Stitch

Row 1 (wrong side): Knit across.
Row 2: Knit across.
Row 3: Change color and Knit across.

Note: Work with 2 strands of yarn throughout.
Note: Edge stitches are not included in stitch instructions, above. See edge stitches, pg. 116.

BACK: With Dk. Blue and size 6 needles, Cast On 85/93/102 sts.
Size 8-10—
Row 1 (wrong side): *Knit 2, Purl 3, Knit 2, Purl 2, Knit 2, Purl 2*. Rep *—* 5 more times. Knit 2, Purl 3, Knit 2.
Size 12-14—
Row 1 (wrong side): Knit 2, Purl 2. Work *—* 6 times (see *—*, size 8-10). Knit 2, Purl 3, Knit 2, Purl 2, Knit 2.
Size 16-18—
Row 1 (wrong side): Purl 2. Work *—* 7 times (see *—*, size 8-10). Knit 2, Purl 3, Knit 2, Purl 2.
Yarn Over Cable & Double Rib—
First row is row 1 of Cable and row 1 of Double Rib.
Size 8-10—
Row 1 (right side): *Purl 2, Slip 1, Knit 2, Psso, Purl 2, Knit 2, Purl 2, Knit 2*. Rep *—* 5 more times. Purl 2, Slip 1, Knit 2, Psso, Purl 2.
Size 12-14—
Row 1 (right side): Purl 2, Knit 2. Work *—* 6 times (see *—*, size 8-10). Purl 2, Slip 1, Knit 2, Psso, Purl 2, Knit 2, Purl 2.
Size 16-18—
Row 1 (right side): Knit 2. Work *—* 7 times (see *—*, size 8-10). Purl 2, Slip 1, Knit 2, Psso, Purl 2, Knit 2.
Sizes 8-10 & 12-14 & 16-18—
Continue to work Double Rib, and rows 1-4 of Cable 5 times.
Stockinette Stitch—
Row 1 (right side): Change to size 8 needles. Knit across and Inc 8/8/7 sts. Inc 1 st on each side edge, remaining 6/6/5

sts evenly across.
Row 2: Knit 1 (edge st), Purl 91/99/107, Knit 1 (edge st).
Fair Isle Pattern—
Row 1: Blue—Knit 2, *Coral—Knit 1, Blue—Knit 3*. Rep *—* 21/23/25 more times. Coral—Knit 1, Blue—Knit 2.
Row 2: Blue—Knit 1, *Coral—Purl 3, Blue—Purl 1*. Rep *—* 21/23/25 more times. Coral—Purl 3, Blue—Knit 1.
Row 3: Same as row 1.
Row 4: Blue—Knit 1, Purl 91/99/107, Knit 1.
Row 5: Knit across.
Row 6: Blue—Knit 1, Purl 1, *Red—Purl 1, Blue—Purl 1*. Rep *—* 43/47/51 more times. Red—Purl 1, Blue—Purl 1, Knit 1.
Row 7: Blue—Knit across.
Row 8: Knit 1, Purl 91/99/107, Knit 1.
Rows 9, 10, 11: Same as rows 1, 2, 3.
Row 12: Blue—Knit 1, Purl 91/99/107, Knit 1.
Row 13: Knit across.
Row 14 (wrong side): Red—Knit across.
Row 15: Knit across.
Row 16 (wrong side): Blue—Knit across.
Row 17: Knit across.
Row 18: Knit 1, Purl 91/99/107, Knit 1.
Rep rows 1-18 three more times. Pattern measures 12 in. (30 cm). Or work to desired length.
Armholes (right side): **Row 1**—Bind Off in Knit 12 sts. Cable—Purl 3 (incl. bind off st), Slip 1, Knit 2, Psso, Purl 2. Fair Isle—continue to work pattern 53/61/69 sts. Cable—Purl 2, Slip 1, Knit 2, Psso, Purl 2. Knit 1. Bind Off remaining 12 sts. Cut yarn. Attach yarn and start next row.
Continue working rows 1-4 of Cable and rows 1-8 of Fair Isle Pattern for 6½/7/7½ in. (16.5/18/19 cm). Bind Off from either right or wrong side.

FRONT: Work same as Back as far as armholes, plus 4½/5/5½ in. (11.5/13/14 cm).
Neck: Work pattern 19/22/25 sts. Bind Off in Knit (or Purl) 31/33/35 sts and work remaining 19/22/25 sts (incl. bind off st).

Shoulders (both stay on needle, but are worked separately): Continue working for 2 in. (5 cm), or to match Back. Bind Off from either right or wrong side.

SHOULDER JOININGS: See pg. 121.

SLEEVES: With Dk. Blue and size 8 needle, from right side, Pick Up 74/79/84 sts (37/39/42 sts on each side, plus 0/1/0 from shoulder seam).

Row 1 (wrong side): Knit across.
Yarn Over Cable—
Row 1: Knit 1, *Purl 2, Slip 1, Knit 2, Psso*. Rep *—* 13/14/15 more times. Purl 2, Knit 1.
Work rows 1-4 of Cable 4 times, plus row 1.
Stockinette Stitch—
Row 1: Knit 1, Purl 72/77/82, Knit 1.
Row 2: Knit and Dec 9 sts evenly across.
Ridge—
Row 1 (wrong side): Red—Knit across.
Row 2: Knit across.
Rows 3, 4: Blue—Knit across.
Row 5: Knit 1, Purl 63/68/73, Knit 1.
Fair Isle—
Work pattern for 15/15¾/16½ in. (38/40/42 cm), or work to desired length.
Stockinette Stitch—
Row 1: Knit across.

Row 2: Purl and Dec 25/26/27 sts evenly across.
Cuffs: Yarn Over Cable & Double Rib—Change to size 6 needles.
First row is row 1 of Cable and row 1 of Double Rib.
Size 8-10—
Row 1: Knit 2, Purl 2, *Knit 2, Purl 2, Knit 2, Purl 2, Slip 1, Knit 2, Psso, Purl 2*. Rep *—*. Knit 2, Purl 2, Knit 2, Purl 2, Knit 2.
Size 12-14—
Row 1: Purl 2, Knit 2, Purl 2. Work *—* twice (see *—*, size 8-10). Knit 2, Purl 2, Knit 2, Purl 2, Knit 2, Purl 2.
Size 16-18—
Row 1: Knit 2, Purl 2, Knit 2, Purl 2. Work *—* twice (see *—*, size 8-10). Knit 2, Purl 2, Knit 2, Purl 2, Knit 2, Purl 2, Knit 2.
Sizes 8-10 & 12-14 & 16-18—
Continue to work Double Rib, and rows 1-4 of Cable 5 times. From right side, Bind Off in Ribbing.

BLOCKING & PRESSING:
See pg. 120.

SEAM JOININGS: See pg. 121.

NECK FINISHING: Reversed Single Crochet in Red. See pg. 123.

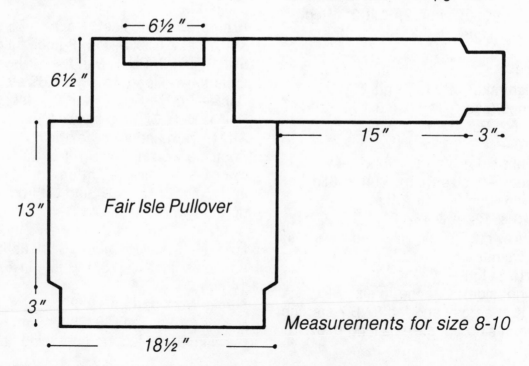

Fair Isle Pullover

6½″

6½″

13″

3″

18½″

15″

3″

Measurements for size 8-10

striped turtleneck

Lightweight wool-blend yarns in two colors are worked into a crisp geometric design. An Uneven Rib alternates with narrow bands of Stockinette and Garter Stitches. The shoulder and neck are paneled in solid white Garter Stitch. The turtleneck, also in Uneven Rib, can be rolled or folded double.

(color photo, page 51)

SIZES: 8-10 / 12-14 / 16-18
For standard sizing, see pg. 11.

MATERIALS: Pingouin "Confortable Fin" (55% acrylic, 45% wool). White and Taupe—5/6/7 skeins each @ 1¾ oz. (50 gr) per skein. Knitting needles size 4 (3.5 mm). Circular needle size 4 (3.5 mm).

GAUGE: Stockinette Stitch, 22 stitches = 4 in. (10 cm).

STITCHES USED: For abbreviations, see pg. 15. For how to knit, see pg. 108.

Uneven Rib_____
Worked over 4 stitches plus 1.
Row 1: Knit 2, Purl 2*. Repeat *—*.
    Knit 1.
    Repeat row 1.

Garter Stitch_____
Knit every row.

Stockinette Stitch_____
Row 1 (right side): Knit across.
Row 2: Purl across.

BACK: With Taupe, Cast On 97/105/117 sts.
Uneven Rib—
Row 1: *Knit 2, Purl 2*. Rep *—* 23/25/28 more times. Knit 1.
Rep row 1 for 3 in. (7.5 cm).
Stockinette & Garter Stitch—
Beginning of repeat.
Row 1 (right side): Taupe—Knit across.

Row 2: Purl across.
Rows 3, 4: White—Knit across.
Rep rows 1-4, plus rows 1, 2.
Uneven Rib—
Row 1 (right side): White—Knit across.
Row 2: *Knit 2, Purl 2*. Rep *—*
23/25/28 more times. Knit 1.
Rep row 2 five more times.
Stockinette & Garter Stitch—
Row 1 (wrong side): Taupe—Purl across.
Row 2: Knit across.
Rows 3, 4: White—Purl across.
Rep rows 1-4, plus rows 1, 2.
Uneven Rib—
Row 1 (wrong side): Taupe—*Knit 2, Purl 2*. Rep *—* 23/25/28 more times. Knit 1.
Rep row 1 eight more times.
Stockinette & Garter Stitch—
Row 1 (right side): Taupe—Knit across.
Row 2: Purl across.
Rows 3, 4: White—Knit across.
Rep rows 1, 2.
Uneven Rib—
Row 1 (right side): White—Knit across.
Row 2: *Knit 2, Purl 2*. Rep *—*
23/25/28 more times. Knit 1.
Rep row 2 five more times.
Stockinette & Garter Stitch—
Row 1 (wrong side): Taupe—Purl across.
Row 2: Knit across.
Rows 3, 4: White—Purl across.
Rep rows 1, 2.
Uneven Rib—
Row 1 (wrong side): Taupe—*Knit 2, Purl 2*. Rep *—* 23/25/28 more times. Knit 1.
Rep row 1 eight more times. End of repeat.
Work pattern repeat 1 more time, plus
1 row of Knit.
Armholes (wrong side): Bind Off in Purl 14 sts. Purl across and Bind Off last 14 sts.
Garter & Stockinette Stitch—
Rows 1, 2: White—Knit across.
Row 3 (right side): Taupe—Knit across.
Row 4: Purl across.
Rep rows 1-4.
Uneven Rib—
Row 1 (right side): White—Knit across.
Row 2: *Knit 2, Purl 2*. Rep *—*
16/18/21 more times. Knit 1.

Rep row 2 five more times.
Stockinette & Garter Stitch—
Row 1 (wrong side): Taupe—Purl across.
Row 2: Knit across.
Rows 3, 4: White—Purl across.
Rep rows 1-4, plus rows 1, 2.
Uneven Rib—
Row 1 (wrong side): Taupe—*Knit 2, Purl 2*. Rep *—* 16/18/21 more times, Knit 1.
Rep row 1 eight more times, plus 1 row of Knit and 1 row of Purl.
Shoulder Panel:
Row 1 (right side): White—Knit across.
Rep row 1 for 5/9/13 more times.
Neck (right side): Knit 15/17/20. Bind Off in Knit 39/43/49 sts. Knit remaining 15/17/20 sts (incl. bind off st).
Shoulders (both stay on needle, but are worked separately): Work Garter Stitch 11 rows, or until armhole length is 6/6½/7 in. (15/16.5/18 cm). Bind Off in Knit.

FRONT: Work same as Back.

SHOULDER JOININGS: See pg. 121.

See pg. 121.

SLEEVES: With White and from right side, Pick Up 69/73/77 sts (34/36/38 sts from each side plus 1 st from shoulder seam). Work Garter Stitch for 2 in. (5 cm), or work to match armhole width.
Stockinette & Garter Stitch—
Beginning of repeat.
Row 1 (wrong side): Taupe—Purl across.
Row 2: Knit across.
Rows 3, 4: White—Purl across.
Rep rows 1, 2.
Uneven Rib—
Row 1 (wrong side): Taupe—*Knit 2, Purl 2*. Rep *—* 16/17/18 more times. Knit 1.
Rep row 1 eight more times.
Stockinette & Garter Stitch—
Row 1 (right side): Taupe—Knit across.
Row 2: Purl across.
Rows 3, 4: White—Knit across.
Rep rows 1, 2.
Uneven Rib—
Row 1 (right side): White—Knit across.
Row 2: *Knit 2, Purl 2*. Rep *—*

16/17/18 more times. Knit 1.
Rep row 2 five more times. End of repeat.
Work pattern repeat 5 times.
Stockinette & Garter Stitch—
Row 1 (wrong side): Taupe—Purl across.
Row 2: Knit across.
Rows 3, 4: White—Purl across.
Row 5: Taupe—Knit across.
Row 6: Purl and Dec 12 sts evenly across.
Cuffs: Work Uneven Rib until sleeve length
is 18/19/20 in. (45.5/48/51 cm), or work
to desired length. From right side, Bind Off
in Ribbing.

BLOCKING & PRESSING:
See pg. 120.

SEAM JOININGS: See pg. 121.

TURTLENECK: From right side, Pick Up
105/113/125 sts around neckline. Place on
circular needle. Work Uneven Rib as on
straight needles for 6 in. (15 cm), or work
to desired length. From wrong side, Bind
Off in Ribbing.

COLLAR FINISHING: From right side,
Whipstitch side edges together.

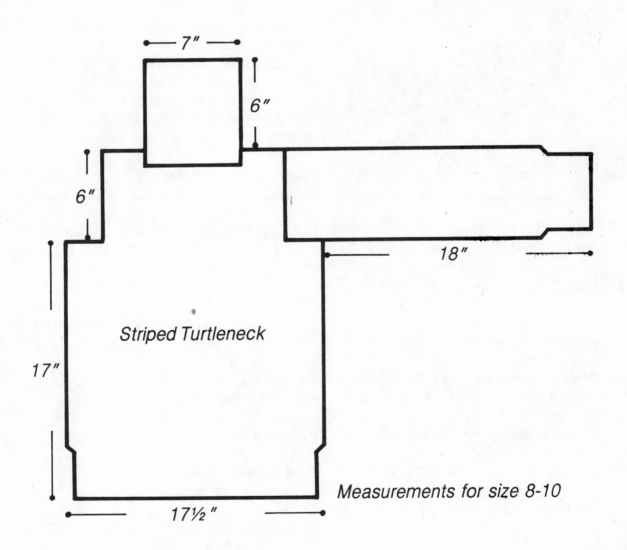

Striped Turtleneck

Measurements for size 8-10

silk tunic

A classic style, worked in a luxurious yarn, becomes a tunic for all occasions. The natural uneven texture of raw silk, combined with the sheen of pearl cotton, creates an elegant effect. This extra-long sweater is slit at each side, and the low V-neck has a semi-shawl collar.

(color photo, page 89)

SIZES: 6-8 / 10-12 / 14-16 / 18
For standard sizing, see pg. 11.

MATERIALS: Lang "Seiden-Bouclé" (80% silk, 20% cotton), imported by Merino Wool. Dk. Natural— 9/10/11/12 skeins @ 1¾ oz. (50 gr) per skein.
DMC "Coton Perlé" No. 5 (100% cotton). Ecru—20/23/25/27 balls @ 53 yd. (48 m) per ball, or silk thread in similar thickness.
DMC "Coton Perlé" No. 5 (100% cotton). Natural—1 skein @ 27.3 yd. (25 m) for seam joinings.
Knitting needles size 8 (5 mm).

GAUGE: Garter Stitch with 2 strands, 16 stitches and 24 rows = 4 in. (10 cm) square.

STITCHES USED: For abbreviations, see pg. 15. For how to knit, see pg. 108.

Garter Stitch_____
Knit every row.

Stockinette Stitch_____
Row 1 (right side): Knit across.
Row 2: Purl across.
Repeat rows 1, 2.

_____
Note: Work with 2 strands of yarn throughout (1 strand of each yarn).

BACK: Cast On 71/77/85/89 sts.
Work Garter Stitch for 7 rows.
Stockinette Stitch & Garter Stitch—
Row 1 (right side): Knit across.
Row 2: Knit 4, Purl 63/69/77/81, Knit 4.
Rep rows 1, 2 two more times.
Rows 7-10: Knit across.
Rep rows 1-10 ten more times, or work to desired length.
Armhole panel:
Row 1: Knit across.
Row 2: Knit 16, Purl 39/45/53/57, Knit 16.
Rep rows 1, 2, plus row 1.
Armholes (wrong side): **Row 6**—Bind Off in Knit 12 sts. Knit 4 (incl. bind off st), Purl 39/45/53/57, Knit 4. Bind Off remaining 12 sts. Cut yarns. Attach yarns and start next row.
Rows 7-10: Knit across.
Rep rows 1-10 two more times, plus row 1.
Neck & Shoulder Panel: Work Garter Stitch until armhole length is 6/6½/7/7½ in. (15/16.5/18/19 cm). From wrong side, Bind Off in Knit.

FRONT: Work same as Back as far as 7 repeats of rows 1-10, plus row 1.
Row 2: Knit 4, Purl 27/30/34/36, Knit 9, Purl 27/30/34/36, Knit 4.
Row 3: Knit across.
Row 4: Knit 4, Purl 27/30/34/36, Knit 4. Bind Off in Knit 1 st. Knit 4, Purl 27/30/34/36, Knit 4.
Row 5: Knit across left Front.
Note: Work each side separately by placing right Front on a separate needle (to be worked later).
Row 6: Knit 4, Purl 27/30/34/36, Knit 4.
Rows 7-10: Knit across.
First pattern change—
Row 1: Knit across.
Row 2: Knit 6, Purl 25/28/32/34, Knit 4.
Rep rows 1, 2 two more times.
Rows 7-10: Knit across.
Second pattern change—
Row 1: Knit across.
Row 2: Knit 8, Purl 23/26/30/32, Knit 4.
Rep rows 1, 2 two more times.
Rows 7-10: Knit across.

Armhole panel: Third pattern change—
Row 1: Knit across.
Row 2: Knit 10, Purl 9/12/16/18, Knit 16.
Rep rows 1, 2, plus row 1.
Armhole (wrong side): **Row 6**—Knit 10, Purl 9/12/16/18, Knit 4. Bind Off in Knit remaining 12 sts.
Rows 7-10: Knit across.
Fourth pattern change—
Row 1: Knit across.
Row 2: Knit 12, Purl 7/10/14/16, Knit 4.
Rep rows 1, 2 two more times.
Rows 7-10: Knit across.
Fifth pattern change—
Row 1: Knit across.
Row 2: Knit 14, Purl 5/8/12/14, Knit 4.
Rep rows 1, 2 two more times.
Rows 7-10: Knit across.
Rep rows 1-10, plus row 1.
Neck & Shoulder Panel: Work Garter Stitch to match Back armhole length.
Shoulder (wrong side): Knit 14. Bind Off in Knit remaining 9/12/16/18 sts.
Collar: Work Garter Stitch for 3½ in. (9 cm). From wrong side, Bind Off in Knit.
Right Front: Work same as left Front, but in reverse.

SHOULDER JOININGS: See pg. 121.

SLEEVES: From right side, Pick Up 48/52/56/60 sts (24/26/28/30 sts on each side of shoulder seam).
Stockinette Stitch—
Row 1 (wrong side): Purl across.
Row 2: Knit across.
Garter Stitch—
Work 16 rows to match armhole width.
Stockinette Stitch & Garter Stitch—
Row 1: Knit across.
Row 2: Knit 4, Purl 40/44/48/52, Knit 4.
Rep rows 1, 2 two more times.
Rows 7-10: Knit across.
Rep rows 1-10 ten more times, plus row 1.
Sleeve Border: Work Garter Stitch until sleeve length is 16¾/17½/18/18¼ in. (42.5/44/45.5/46 cm), or work to desired length. From wrong side, Bind Off in Knit.

BLOCKING & PRESSING:
See pg. 120.

SEAM JOININGS: See pg. 121.

COLLAR FINISHING: From right side,
Whipstitch back edges of collar together.
Attach seam to center of sweater Back,
and Whipstitch edges of collar and sweater
together.

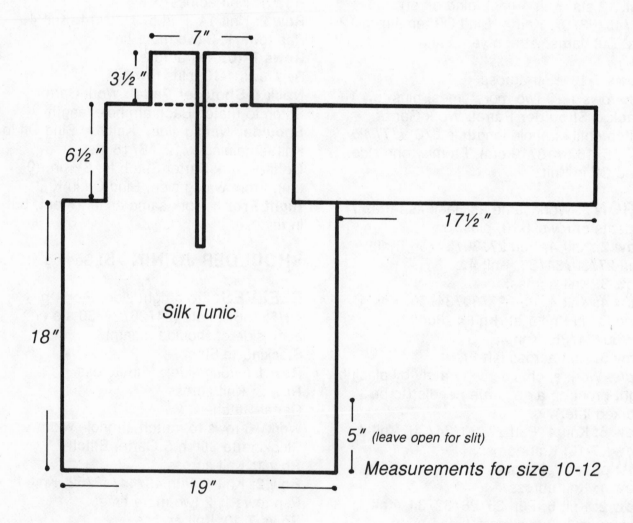

7"

3½"

6½"

17½"

18"

Silk Tunic

5" (leave open for slit)

Measurements for size 10-12

19"

hooded cardigan

A unique combination of stitches gives a fitted, yet elastic, shape to this zippered sweater in vivid orange-red wool. The body and sleeves are worked in alternating rows of Trinity Stitch and Cables. Cuffs and hood are in solid clusters of Trinity Stitch.

(color photo, page 69)

SIZES: 8-10 / 12-14
   For standard sizing, see pg. 11.

MATERIALS: ''Persian Crewel Wool'' (100% wool), or a quality knitting worsted. Orange-red—5 skeins @ 8 oz. (225 gr) per skein. Knitting needles size 6 (4 mm). Circular needle size 6 (4 mm). Orange separating zipper, 23 in. (57 cm).

GAUGE: Pattern Stitches, 22 stitches = 4 in. (10 cm).

STITCHES USED: For abbreviations, see pg. 15. For how to knit, see pg. 108.

Double Rib
Worked over 4 stitches plus 2.
Row 1: *Knit 2, Purl 2*. Repeat *—*. Knit 2.
Row 2: *Purl 2, Knit 2*. Repeat *—*. Purl 2.
   Repeat rows 1, 2.

Yarn Over Cable
Worked over 3 stitches plus 4.
Row 1 (right side): Purl 2, Slip 1, Knit 2, Psso, Purl 2.
Row 2: Knit 2, Purl 1, Yo, Purl 1, Knit 2.
Row 3: Purl 2, Knit 3, Purl 2.
Row 4: Knit 2, Purl 3, Knit 2.
   Repeat rows 1-4.
Note: All Slip Stitches are slipped purlwise with yarn in back.

Trinity Stitch_____

Worked over 4 stitches plus 2.

Row 1 (wrong side): Knit 1, Knit 1/Purl 1/Knit 1 into one stitch, Purl 3 together, Knit 1.

Row 2: Purl across.

Row 3: Knit 1, Purl 3 together, Knit 1/Purl 1/Knit 1 into one stitch, Knit 1.

Row 4: Purl across.

Repeat rows 1-4.

BACK: Cast On 110/122 sts.

Double Rib & Cable—

Additional stitches for size 12-14 are in parenthesis.

First row worked is row 2 of Double Rib and row 4 of Cable.

Row 1 (wrong side): (Knit 2, Purl 2, Knit 2), *Purl 2, Knit 2, Purl 2, Knit 2, Purl 3, Knit 2*. Rep *—* 7 more times. Purl 2, Knit 2, Purl 2, (Knit 2, Purl 2, Knit 2).

Double Rib & Cable—

Row 1 (right side): (Purl 2, Knit 2, Purl 2), *Knit 2, Purl 2, Knit 2, Purl 2, Slip 1, Knit 2, Psso, Purl 2*. Rep *—* 7 more times. Knit 2, Purl 2, Knit 2, (Purl 2, Knit 2, Purl 2).

Row 2: (Knit 2, Purl 2, Knit 2), *Purl 2, Knit 2, Purl 2, Knit 2, Purl 1, Yo, Purl 1, Knit 2*. Rep *—* 7 more times. Purl 2, Knit 2, Purl 2, (Knit 2, Purl 2, Knit 2).

Row 3: (Purl 2, Knit 2, Purl 2), *Knit 2, Purl 2, Knit 2, Purl 2, Knit 3, Purl 2*. Rep *—* 7 more times. Knit 2, Purl 2, Knit 2, (Purl 2, Knit 2, Purl 2).

Row 4: (Knit 2, Purl 2, Knit 2), *Purl 2, Knit 2, Purl 2, Knit 2, Purl 3, Knit 2*. Rep *—* 7 more times. Purl 2, Knit 2, Purl 2, (Knit 2, Purl 2, Knit 2).

Rep rows 1-4 for 7½ in. (19 cm), plus row 1 (12 Cables).

Cable & Trinity Stitch (Double Rib is replaced by Trinity Stitch)—

Row 1 (wrong side): (Knit 6), Knit 1, *Knit/Purl/Knit into one stitch, Purl 3 tog, Knit 3, Purl 1, Yo, Purl 1, Knit 3*. Rep *—* 7 more times. Knit/Purl/Knit into one stitch, Purl 3 tog, Knit 1, (Knit 6).

Row 2: (Purl 6), Purl 8, *Knit 3, Purl 10*. Rep *—* 6 more times. Knit 3, Purl 8, (Purl 6).

Row 3: (Knit 6), Knit 1, *Purl 3 tog, Knit/Purl/Knit into one stitch, Knit 3, Purl 3, Knit 3*. Rep *—* 7 more times. Purl 3 tog, Knit/Purl/Knit into one stitch, Knit 1, (Knit 6).

Fourth row worked is row 2 of Trinity Stitch and row 1 of Cable.

Row 4: (Purl 6), Purl 8, *Slip 1, Knit 2, Psso, Purl 10*. Rep *—* 6 more times. Slip 1, Knit 2, Psso, Purl 8, (Purl 6).

Rep rows 1-4 for 9½ in. (24 cm), or 15 Cables (27 Cables altogether).

Note: Always Bind Off on row 2 of Cable. Omit Yo when Binding Off.

Armholes: From wrong side, Bind Off in Knit 12 sts. Work pattern. Bind Off last 12 sts. Cut yarn. Attach yarn and start next row. Continue working for 5¾/6¼ in. (14.5/16 cm), or 11/12 Cables (38/39 Cables altogether).

Neck (wrong side): Cable row 2—Work pattern 21/25 sts. Bind Off 38/44 sts and work remaining 21/25 sts (incl. bind off st).

Shoulders (both stay on needle, but are worked separately): Work one more Cable. From wrong side and row 2 of Cable, Bind Off in Knit.

RIGHT FRONT: Cast On 55/61 sts.

Double Rib & Cable—

Additional stitches for size 12-14 are in parenthesis.

First row worked is row 2 of Double Rib and row 4 of Cable.

Row 1 (wrong side): (Knit 2, Purl 2, Knit 2), *Purl 2, Knit 2, Purl 2, Knit 2, Purl 3, Knit 2*. Rep *—* 3 more times. Purl 2, Knit 1.

Double Rib & Cable—

Row 1: Purl 1, Knit 2, *Purl 2, Slip 1, Knit 2, Psso, Purl 2, Knit 2, Purl 2, Knit 2*. Rep *—* 3 more times. (Purl 2, Knit 2, Purl 2).

Row 2: (Knit 2, Purl 2, Knit 2), *Purl 2, Knit 2, Purl 2, Knit 2, Purl 1, Yo, Purl 1, Knit 2*. Rep *—* 3 more times. Purl 2, Knit 1.

Row 3: Purl 1, Knit 2, *Purl 2, Knit 3, Purl 2, Knit 2, Purl 2, Knit 2*. Rep *—* 3 more times. (Purl 2, Knit 2, Purl 2).

Row 4: (Knit 2, Purl 2, Knit 2), *Purl 2, Knit 2, Purl 2, Knit 2, Purl 3, Knit 2*. Rep

— 3 more times. Purl 2, Knit 1.
Continue working pattern rows 1-4 for 7½
in. (19 cm), plus row 1 (12 Cables).
Cable & Trinity Stitch—
Row 1 (wrong side): (Knit 6), Knit 1,
*Knit/Purl/Knit into one stitch, Purl 3 tog,
Knit 3, Purl 1, Yo, Purl 1, Knit 3*. Rep *—*
2 more times. Knit/Purl/Knit into one
stitch, Purl 3 tog, Knit 3, Purl 1, Yo, Purl 1,
Knit 2, Purl 2, Knit 1.
Row 2: Purl 1, Knit 2, Purl 2, *Knit 3,
Purl 10*. Rep *—* 2 more times. Knit 3,
Purl 8, (Purl 6).
Row 3: (Knit 6), Knit 1, *Purl 3 tog,
Knit/Purl/Knit into one stitch, Knit 3,
Purl 3, Knit 3*. Rep *—* 2 more times.
Knit/Purl/Knit into one stitch, Purl 3 tog,
Knit 3, Purl 3, Knit 2, Purl 2, Knit 1.
Row 4: Purl 1, Knit 2, Purl 2, *Slip 1, Knit
2, Psso, Purl 10*. Rep *—* 2 more times.
Slip 1, Knit 2, Psso, Purl 8, (Purl 6).
Continue working pattern rows 1-4 for 9½
in. (24 cm), or 15 Cables (27 Cables al-
together). End on Cable row 1.
Note: Always Bind Off on row 2 of Cable.
Omit Yo when Binding Off.
Armhole: From wrong side, Bind Off in Knit
12 sts. Work pattern 42/49 sts (incl. bind
off st). Continue working for 4¾/5¼ in.
(12/13.5 cm), or 10/11 Cables (37/38
altogether).
Neck (wrong side): Cable row 2—Work pattern 21/25 sts. Bind Off in Knit 16/19 sts.
Work remaining 3 sts (incl. bind off st).
Place sts on safety pin. Cut yarn. Attach
yarn and start next row.
Shoulder: Work two more Cables, or work
to match Back armhole length. From wrong
side and row 2 of Cable, Bind Off in Knit.

LEFT FRONT: Work same as right
Front, but in reverse.
Row 1 (wrong side): Knit 1, Purl 2, *Knit 2,
Purl 3, Knit 2, Purl 2, Knit 2, Purl 2*. Rep
— 3 more times. (Knit 2, Purl 2, Knit 2).

SHOULDER JOININGS: See pg. 121.

SLEEVES: From right side, Pick Up
76/82 sts (38/41 sts on each side of
shoulder seam).
Cable & Trinity Stitch—
First row worked is row 4 of Cable and row
3 of Trinity Stitch.
Row 1 (wrong side): (Knit 3), Purl 2, Knit 2,
*Purl 3 , Knit 3, Purl 3 tog, Knit/Purl/Knit
into one stitch, Knit 3*. Rep *—* 4 more
times. Purl 3, Knit 2, Purl 2, (Knit 3).
Row 2: (Purl 3), Knit 2, Purl 2, *Slip 1, Knit
2, Psso, Purl 10*. Rep *—* 4 more times.
Slip 1, Knit 2, Psso, Purl 2, Knit 2, (Purl 3).
Row 3: (Knit 3), Purl 2, Knit 2, *Purl 1, Yo,
Purl 1, Knit 3, Knit/Purl/Knit into one
stitch, Purl 3 tog, Knit 3*. Rep *—* 4 more
times. Purl 1, Yo, Purl 1, Knit 2, Purl 2,
(Knit 3).
Row 4: (Purl 3), Knit 2, Purl 2, *Knit 3, Purl
10*. Rep *—* 4 more times. Knit 3, Purl 2,
Knit 2, (Purl 3).
Continue working pattern rows until sleeve
length is 16½ in. (42 cm), or 28 Cables
from armhole. End on Cable row 1.
Cuffs: Dec 6 sts across row (omit all Yo).
At the same time, replace Cable with Trinity
Stitch.
Row 1 (wrong side): Knit 1/4, Purl 3 tog,
Knit/Purl/Knit into one stitch, omit Yo, Purl
3 tog, Knit/Purl/Knit into one stitch, *Purl
3 tog, Knit/Purl/Knit into one stitch, Purl 3
tog, Knit/Purl/Knit into one stitch, omit Yo,
Purl 3 tog, Knit/Purl/Knit into one stitch*.
Rep *—* 4 more times. Knit 1/4.
Row 2: Purl across.
Row 3: Knit 1/4, *Knit/Purl/Knit into one
stitch, Purl 3 tog*. Rep *—* 16 more
times. Knit 1/4.
Row 4: Purl across.
Continue working Trinity Stitch for 2½/3½
in. (6.5/9 cm).

BLOCKING & PRESSING:
See pg. 120.

SEAM JOININGS: See pg. 121.

HOOD: Right side of right Front—Place the 3 sts from safety pin onto circular needle. Pick Up 106/114 sts. Work remaining 3 sts from left Front onto circular needle.

Row 1 (wrong side): Knit 1, Purl 110/118, Knit 1. Turn.

Row 2: Knit across. Turn.

Trinity Stitch—

Row 1 (wrong side): Knit 1, Purl 2, Knit 1, *Knit/Purl/Knit into one stitch, Purl 3 tog*. Rep *—* 25/27 more times. Knit 1, Purl 2, Knit 1.

Row 2: Purl 1, Knit 2, Purl 106/114, Knit 2, Purl 1.

Row 3: Knit 1, Purl 2, Knit 1, *Purl 3 tog, Knit/Purl/Knit into one stitch*. Rep *—* 25/27 more times. Knit 1, Purl 2, Knit 1.

Row 4: Purl 1, Knit 2, Purl 106/114, Knit 2, Purl 1.

Continue working rows 1-4 for 13 in. (33 cm). From wrong side, Bind Off in Knit.

HOOD & FRONT FINISHING: With wrong side inside, fold hood in half. From right side, Whipstitch together (see pg. 121).

Carefully pin and attach zipper to both Front edges.

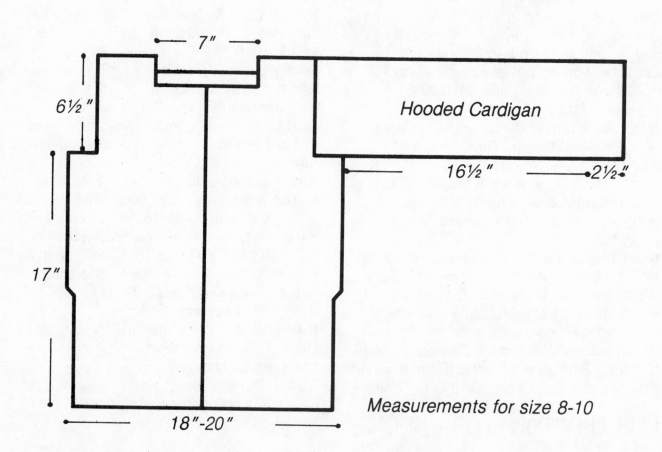

7"

6½"

Hooded Cardigan

16½"   2½"

17"

18"-20"

Measurements for size 8-10

70   *Super Sweater, page 78*   *Multicolored Pullover, page 75*

Trinity Stitch Cardigan, page 80

warm wrap coat

Two colors and two stitches pattern this short coat. One strand each of pale coral and natural in a wool-blend yarn gives a soft tweed look, as well as extra warmth. The roomy body and sleeves are in Double Rib. The cuffs, panels and stand-up collar are in Garter Stitch.

SIZES: 8-10 / 12-14 / 16-18
For standard sizing, see pg. 11.

MATERIALS: Coats & Clark "Bulky Loop" (60% wool, 40% polyester). Natural and Lt. Coral—16/17/18 skeins each @ 1¾ oz. (50 gr) per skein.
Knitting needles size 10½ (6.5 mm).
Circular needle size 10½ (6.5 mm).

GAUGE: Garter Stitch with 2 strands, 12 stitches = 4 in. (10 cm).

STITCHES USED: For abbreviations, see pg. 15. For how to knit, see pg. 108.

Garter Stitch_____
Knit every row.

Double Rib_____
Worked over 4 stitches plus 2.
Row 1: *Knit 2, Purl 2*. Repeat *—*. Knit 2.
Row 2: *Purl 2, Knit 2*. Repeat *—*. Purl 2.
Repeat rows 1, 2.

_____
Note: Work with 2 strands of yarn throughout (1 strand of each color).

BACK: Cast On 58/62/66 sts and work Garter Stitch for 2 in. (5 cm).
Double Rib—
Row 1 (right side): *Knit 2, Purl 2*. Rep *—* 13/14/15 more times. Knit 2.
Row 2: *Purl 2, Knit 2*. Rep *—* 13/14/15 more times. Purl 2.
Rep rows 1, 2 for 18 in. (46 cm), or work to desired length.
Garter Stitch & Double Rib—
Row 1 (right side): Knit 16, work Double Rib for 26/30/34 sts, Knit remaining 16 sts. Continue working pattern for 2 in. (5 cm).
Armholes (right side): Bind Off in Knit 8 sts. Work pattern and Bind Off last 8 sts. Cut yarns. Attach yarns and start next row. Continue working until armhole length is 5/5½/6 in. (12.5/14/15 cm).
Shoulder Panel: Work Garter Stitch for 3 in. (7.5 cm).
Neck & Shoulders: Bind Off in Knit 11/12/13 sts. Place 20/22/24 sts on safety pin (incl. bind off st). Bind Off remaining 11/12/13 sts.

RIGHT FRONT: Cast On 36/40/44 sts and work Garter Stitch for 2 in. (5 cm).
Front Border & Double Rib—
Row 1 (right side): Knit 10, *Knit 2, Purl 2*. Rep *—* 5/6/7 more times. Knit 2.
Row 2: *Purl 2, Knit 2*. Rep *—* 5/6/7 more times. Purl 2, Knit 10.
Rep rows 1, 2 for 18 in. (46 cm), or work to match Back.
Double Rib & Garter Stitch—
Row 1 (right side): Knit 10, *Knit 2, Purl 2*. Rep *—* 1/2/3 more times. Knit 18.
Row 2: Knit 16, *Purl 2, Knit 2*. Rep *—* 1/2/3 more times. Purl 2, Knit 10.
Continue working pattern for 2 in. (5 cm).
Armhole (right side): Work pattern and Bind Off in Knit last 8 sts. Cut yarns. Attach yarns and start next row.
Continue working until armhole length is

4/4½/5 in. (10/11.5/12.5 cm), or work to match Back.

Shoulder Panel: Work Garter Stitch for 2 in. (5 cm).

Neck (right side): Place 19/20/21 sts on safety pin. Knit remaining 9/12/15 sts.

Shoulder: Continue working for 2 in. (5 cm), or work to match Back armhole length. Bind Off in Knit.

LEFT FRONT: Work same as right Front, but in reverse.

SHOULDER JOININGS: See pg. 121.

SLEEVES: From wrong side and 2 sts in from edge, Pick Up 46/50/54 sts (23/25/27 sts on each side of shoulder seam).

Double Rib—

Row 1 (right side): *Knit 2, Purl 2*. Rep *—* 10/11/12 more times. Knit 2.

Row 2: *Purl 2, Knit 2*. Rep *—* 10/11/12 more times. Purl 2.

Rep rows 1, 2 until sleeve length is 16/17/18 in. (40.5/43/45.5 cm).

Cuffs: Work Garter Stitch for 4 in. (10 cm), or work to desired length. Bind Off in Knit.

BLOCKING & PRESSING:
See pg. 120.

SEAM JOININGS: See pg. 121.

COLLAR:
From right side, Knit stitches from right Front safety pin onto circular needle. Pick Up 9 sts. Knit stitches from Back safety pin. Pick Up 9 sts. Knit stitches from left Front safety pin. Work Garter Stitch as on straight needles for 3 in. (7.5 cm), or work to desired width. Bind Off in Knit.

FINISHING: Turn cuffs to right side.

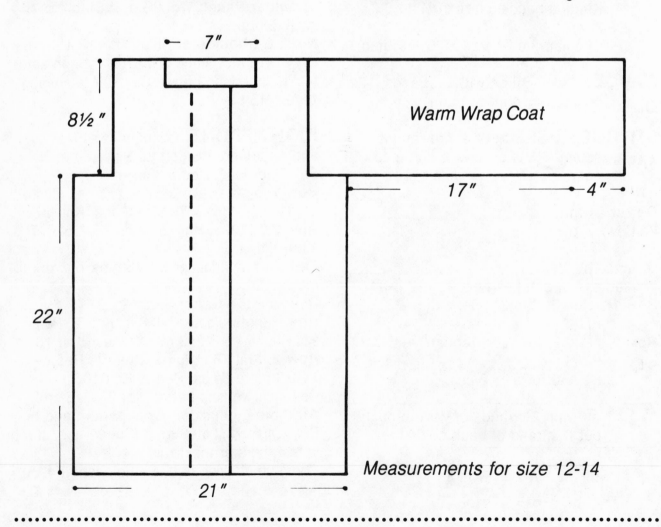

7"

8½"

Warm Wrap Coat

17" 4"

22"

21"

Measurements for size 12-14

multicolored pullover

Here's a classic shape. Stripes of beige, pink and green form horizontal bands against a camel background. The pure wool yarn is worked in a unique combination of Stockinette and Garter Stitches. Single Ribbing fashions the narrow, overlapping shawl collar, as well as the waist and cuffs.

(color photo, page 70)

SIZES: 34-36 / 38-40 / 42-44 / 46-48
For standard sizing, see pg. 11.

MATERIALS: ''Persian Crewel Wool''
(100% wool). Lt. Beige—11½ /
12/12½ /13 oz. (322/336/350/
364 gr). Camel—14½ /15/15½ /16
oz. (406/420/434/448 gr). Pink,
Lt. Pink and Lt. Green—3½ /4 /
4½ /5 oz. (98/112/126/140 gr)
each.
Knitting needles size 6 (4 mm).
Circular needle size 6 (4 mm).

GAUGE: Stockinette Stitch, 18 stitches
and 24 rows = 4 in. (10 cm)
square.
16 rows

STITCHES USED: For abbreviations,
see pg. 15. For how to knit, see
pg. 108.

Single Rib_____
Worked over 2 stitches.
Row 1: *Knit 1, Purl 1*. Repeat *—*.
Row 2: *Knit 1, Purl 1*. Repeat *—*.
Repeat rows 1, 2.

Stockinette Stitch_____
Row 1 (right side): Knit across.
Row 2: Purl across.
Repeat rows 1, 2.

Garter Stitch_____
Knit every row.

BACK: With Lt. Beige, Cast On 94/102/110/118 sts and work Single Rib for 2½ in. (6.5 cm).
Stockinette Stitch—
Row 1 (right side): Knit across.
Row 2: Purl across.
Rep rows 1, 2.
Stripe Pattern—
Rows 1-3: Camel—Knit across.
Rows 4-6: Purl across.
Rows 7, 8: Knit across.
Row 9 (right side): Lt. Beige—Knit across.
Row 10: Purl across.
Row 11 (right side): Lt. Green—Knit across.
Row 12: Purl across.
Row 13: Knit across.
Row 14 (wrong side): Lt. Pink—Knit across.
Row 15: Knit across.
Row 16: Purl across.
Row 17 (right side): Pink—Purl across.
Row 18: Purl across.
Row 19: Knit across.
Row 20 (wrong side): Lt. Beige—Purl across.
Row 21: Knit across.
Rows 22-24: Camel—Purl across.
Rows 25-27: Knit across.
Rows 28, 29: Purl across.
Row 30 (wrong side): Lt. Beige—Purl across.
Row 31: Knit across.
Row 32 (wrong side): Lt. Green—Purl across.
Row 33: Knit across.
Row 34: Purl across.
Row 35 (right side): Lt. Pink—Purl across.
Row 36: Purl across.
Row 37: Knit across.
Row 38 (wrong side): Pink—Knit across.
Row 39: Knit across.
Row 40: Purl across.
Row 41 (right side): Lt. Beige—Knit across.
Row 42: Purl across.
Rep rows 1-42 two more times, or work to desired length.

Ridge Pattern—
Row 1 (right side): Camel—Knit across.
Rows 2, 3: Knit across.
Row 4 (wrong side): Purl across.
Rows 5, 6: Purl across.
Rep rows 1, 2.
Armholes (right side): **Row 3**—Bind Off in Knit 15 sts. Knit 64/72/80/88 (incl. bind off st). Bind Off remaining 15 sts. Cut yarn. Attach yarn and start next row.
Continue working rows 4-6 and 1-3 until armhole length is 8/8½/9/9½ in. (20/21.5/23/24.5 cm).
Neck: Work 16/18/20/22 sts. Bind Off in Knit 32/36/40/44 sts. Work remaining 16/18/20/22 sts (incl. bind off st).
Shoulders (both stay on needle, but are worked separately): Work Ridge Pattern for ½ in. (1.3 cm). From right side, Bind Off in Knit.

FRONT: Work same as Back as far as armholes.
Armholes (right side): **Row 3**—Bind Off in Knit 15 sts. Knit 25/29/33/37 (incl. bind off st). Bind Off 14 sts. Knit 25/29/33/37 (incl. bind off st). Bind Off remaining 15 sts. Cut yarn. Attach yarn and start next row.
Note: Work each side separately by placing left side on a separate needle (to be worked later).
Continue working rows 4-6.
Row 1 (right side): Neck opening—Dec 1 st (Knit 2 tog), Knit remaining 23/27/31/35.
Rows 2-4: Work pattern.
Row 5: Dec 1 st (Purl 2 tog), Purl remaining 22/26/30/34 sts.
Note: Dec 1 st every fourth row until 16/18/20/22 sts remain (Dec 9/11/13/15 altogether).
Continue working Ridge Pattern to match Back armhole length.
Left side: Work same as right side, but in reverse.

SHOULDER JOININGS: See pg. 121.

SLEEVES: With Camel and from right side, Pick Up 68/72/76/80 sts (34/36/38/40 sts on each side of shoulder seam).
Ridge Pattern—
Rows 1, 2: Knit across.
Rows 3-5: Purl across.
Rows 6, 7: Knit across.
Stripe Pattern—
First row is row 9 of pattern (see Back). Continue working Stripe Pattern, reversing Lt. Green and Pink to match sweater body. Starting on middle ridge of third Camel stripe, Dec 1 st on both edges. Rep on next 4 Camel stripes (Dec 10 sts altogether). Work until sleeve length is 16½/17½/18½/19 in. (42/44.5/47/48 cm). Dec 13 sts across last row.
Cuffs: Work Single Rib for 5 in. (12.5 cm). From wrong side, Bind Off in Ribbing.

BLOCKING & PRESSING:
See pg. 120.

SEAM JOININGS: See pg. 121.

COLLAR: With Lt. Beige and on right side of right Front, Pick Up 136/144/152/160 sts around neckline. Place on circular needle and work Single Rib as on straight needles for 3 in. (7.5 cm). From wrong side, Bind Off in Ribbing.

FINISHING: Overlap front edges of collar and attach to center opening.

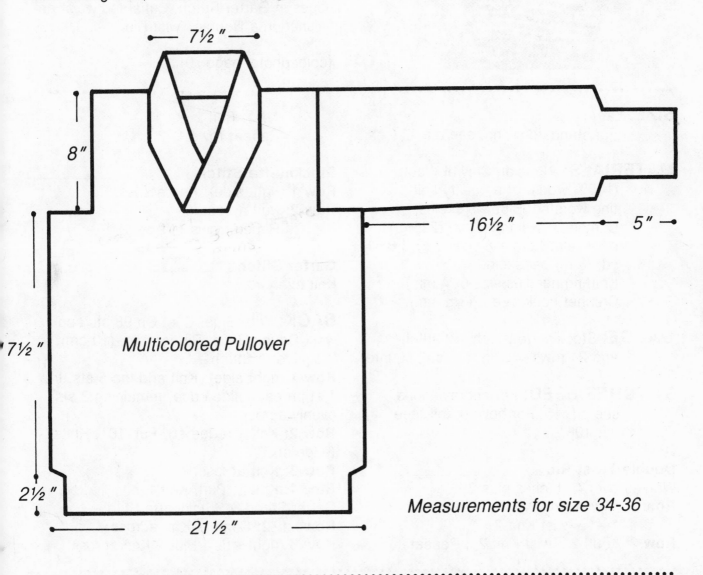

7½ "

8 "

7½ "

2½ "

21½ "

16½ "

5 "

Multicolored Pullover

Measurements for size 34-36

super sweater

A pure wool sweater goes to extra lengths to cover. The solid blue areas in Stockinette Stitch are brightened with striped ridges in Garter Stitch. Cuffs and waist are finished in a Double Twist Rib.

(color photo, page 70)

SIZE: Large
For standard sizing, see pg. 11.

MATERIALS: ''Persian Crewel Wool'' (100% wool), or a quality knitting worsted. Blue—3 skeins; Camel—1 skein @ 8 oz. (225 gr) per skein. Coral—8 skeins @ 8.8 yd. (8 m) per skein. Knitting needles size 6 (4 mm). Crochet hook size E (3.5 mm).

GAUGE: Stockinette Stitch, 18 stitches and 24 rows = 4 in. (10 cm) square.

STITCHES USED: For abbreviations, see pg. 15. For how to knit, see pg. 108.

Double Twist Rib_____
Worked over 4 stitches plus 2.
Row 1: *Twist Knit 2, Purl 2*. Repeat *—*. Twist Knit 2.
Row 2: *Purl 2, Twist Knit 2*. Repeat *—*. Purl 2.
Repeat rows 1, 2.

Stockinette Stitch_____
Row 1 (right side): Knit across.
Row 2: Purl across.
Repeat rows 1, 2.

Garter Stitch_____
Knit every row.

BACK: With Blue, Cast On 98 sts and work Double Twist Rib for 4 in. (10 cm). Stockinette Stitch—
Row 1 (right side): Knit and Inc 5 sts. Inc 1 st on each side edge, remaining 3 sts evenly across.
Row 2: Knit 1 (edge st), Purl 101, Knit 1 (edge st).
Row 3: Knit across.
Row 4: Knit 1, Purl, Knit 1.
Garter Stitch & Stockinette Stitch—
Rows 1, 2: Camel—Knit across.
Row 3 (right side): Blue—Knit across.

Row 4: Knit 1, Purl, Knit 1.
Rep rows 3, 4.
Rows 7, 8: Camel—Knit across.
Rows 9-12: Blue—Same as rows 3-6.
Rows 13, 14: Camel—Knit across.
Rows 15-18: Blue—Same as rows 3-6.
Rows 19, 20: Coral—Knit across.
Rows 21-24: Blue—Same as rows 3-6.
Rep rows 1-24 three more times, plus rows 1-23. Or work to desired length.
Armholes (wrong side): **Row 24**—Bind Off 22 sts, Purl 59 (incl. bind off st). Bind Off remaining 22 sts. Cut yarn. Attach yarn and start next row. Continue working rows 1-24, plus rows 1-12, plus rep rows 13, 14 four times.
Neck (right side): Knit 15, Bind Off in Knit 29 sts, Knit 15 (incl. bind off st).
Shoulders (both stay on needle, but are worked separately): Work 4 more rows of Garter Stitch. From wrong side, Bind Off in Knit. Armhole length is 7¼ in. (18.5 cm).

FRONT: Work same as Back.

SHOULDER JOININGS: See pg. 121.

SLEEVES: With Camel and from right side, Pick Up 64 sts (32 sts on each side of shoulder seam).
Garter Stitch—
Rows 1-13: Knit across.
Garter Stitch & Stockinette Stitch—
Continue working pattern rows 3-24. Work rows 1-24 three times, plus rows 1-17. Sleeve length is 14 in. (35.5 cm). Or work to desired length.
Row 18: Purl and Dec 22 sts evenly across.
Cuffs: Work Double Twist Rib for 4 in. (10 cm). Bind Off in Ribbing.

BLOCKING & PRESSING: See pg. 120.

SEAM JOININGS: See pg. 121.

NECK FINISHING: With Camel, work Reversed Single Crochet. See pg. 123.

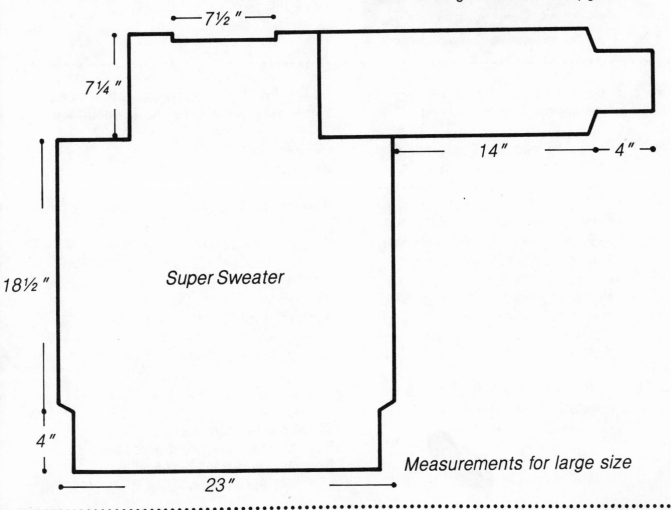

7½"

7¼"

14"   4"

18½"

4"

Super Sweater

Measurements for large size

23"

trinity stitch cardigan

A tricolored, striped cardigan in muted tones has sleeves worked in solid clusters of Trinity Stitch. Shoulders are accented with the same mauve mohair stripes that separate the wider body sections. An Uneven Ribbing fashions the waist and the cuffs.

(color photo, page 71)

SIZES: 6-8 / 10-12 / 14-16 / 18
For standard sizing, see pg. 11.

MATERIALS: Pingouin ''Confortable'' (55% wool, 45% acrylic). Gray—4/5/6 skeins; Blue—7/8/9 skeins @ 1¾ oz. (50 gr) per skein. Chat Botté ''Chaleureuse'' (40% mohair, 40% wool, 20% vinyon). Mauve—2/3/3 skeins @ 1²/₅ oz. (40 gr) per skein.
Knitting needles size 4 (3.5 mm) and size 6 (4 mm).
Circular needle size 6 (4 mm).
7 buttons.

GAUGE: Stockinette Stitch and size 6 needles, 20 stitches = 4 in. (10 cm).

STITCHES USED: For abbreviations, see pg. 15. For how to knit, see pg. 108.

Uneven Rib_____
Worked over 4 stitches plus 1.
Row 1: *Knit 2, Purl 2*. Repeat *—*.
Knit 1.
Repeat row 1.

Single Rib_____
Worked over 2 stitches plus 1.
Row 1: *Knit 1, Purl 1*. Repeat *—*.
Knit 1.
Row 2: *Purl 1, Knit 1*. Repeat *—*.
Purl 1.
Repeat rows 1, 2.

Stockinette Stitch_____
Row 1 (right side): Knit across.
Row 2: Purl across.
Repeat rows 1, 2.

Trinity Stitch_____

Worked over 4 stitches plus 2.

Row 1 (wrong side): Knit 1, *Knit 1/Purl 1/ Knit 1 into one stitch, Purl 3 together*. Repeat *—*. Knit 1.

Row 2: Purl across.

Row 3: Knit 1, *Purl 3 together, Knit 1/ Purl 1/Knit 1 into one stitch*. Repeat *—*. Knit 1.

Row 4: Purl across.
Repeat rows 1-4.

BACK: With Gray and size 4 needles,
Cast On 85/89/97/101 sts. Work Uneven Rib for 3½ in. (9 cm).

Stockinette Stitch—Change to size 6 needles.

Row 1 (right side): Knit across and Inc 10/14/14/14 sts. Inc 1 st on each side edge, remaining 8/12/12/12 sts evenly across.

Row 2: Purl 95/103/111/115.

Stripe & Trinity Stitch Pattern—

Row 1 (right side): Mauve—Knit across.

Row 2: Knit across.

Row 3: Gray—Knit across.

Row 4: Purl across.

Row 5: Knit across.

Row 6 (wrong side): Blue—Knit 1, *Knit/Purl/Knit into one st, Purl 3 tog*. Rep *—* 22/24/26/27 more times. Knit/Purl/Knit into one stitch, Knit 1.

Row 7: Purl across.

Row 8: Knit 1, *Purl 3 tog, Knit/Purl/Knit into one stitch*. Rep *—* 22/24/26/27 more times. Purl 3 tog, Knit 1.

Row 9: Purl across.
Rep rows 6-8.

Row 13: Gray—Knit across.

Row 14: Purl across.
Rep rows 1-14 four more times, plus rows 1-5.

Trinity Stitch—

Row 1: Same as row 6.

Row 2: Purl across.

Row 3: Same as row 8.

Row 4: Purl across.
Rep row 1.

Armholes (right side): **Row 2**—Bind Off in Purl 15 sts. Work pattern 65/73/81/85 sts (incl. bind off st). Bind Off remaining 15 sts. Cut yarn. Attach yarn and start next row. Continue working Trinity Stitch until armhole length is 6/6½/7/7½ in. (15/16.5/ 18/19 cm).

Neck & Shoulders: From right side, Bind Off in Purl 11/15/19/21 sts. Place 43 sts on a safety pin (incl. bind off st). Bind Off remaining 11/15/19/21 sts.

LEFT FRONT: Cast On 41/43/47/49
sts and work Uneven Rib for 3½ in. (9 cm).

Stockinette Stitch—

Row 1 (right side): Knit across and Inc 5/7/7/9 sts. Inc 1 st on side edge, remaining 4/6/6/8 sts evenly across.

Row 2: Purl 46/50/54/58.

Stripe & Trinity Stitch Pattern—

Rows 1-5: Same as Back.

Row 6 (wrong side): Blue—Knit 1, *Purl 3 tog, Knit/Purl/Knit into one st*. Rep *—* 10/11/12/13 more times. Knit 1.

Row 7: Purl across.

Row 8: Knit 1, *Knit/Purl/Knit into one st, Purl 3 tog*. Rep *—* 10/11/12/13 more times. Knit 1.

Row 9: Purl across.
Rep rows 6-8.

Rows 13, 14: Same as Back.
Rep rows 1-14 four more times, plus rows 1-5. ▷

Trinity Stitch—
Row 1: Same as row 6.
Row 2: Purl across.
Row 3: Dec 1 st (Purl 2 tog), Purl 3 tog, continue Trinity Stitch across.
Row 4: Purl across.
Rep row 1.
Armhole (right side): **Row 2**—Bind Off in Purl 15 sts. Purl across.
Row 3: Dec 1 st (Purl 4 tog), Knit/Purl/Knit into one st, continue Trinity Stitch across.
Note: Dec 10 sts, one st on every row 3 of Trinity Stitch, or until 11/15/19/21 sts remain.
Continue working Trinity Stitch to match Back armhole length.

RIGHT FRONT: Work same as left Front, but in reverse.

SHOULDER JOININGS: see pg. 121.

SLEEVES: With Blue and size 6 needle, from right side, Pick Up 67/7l/75/79 sts (33/35/37/39 sts on each side, plus 1 st from shoulder seam).
Row 1 (wrong side): Purl across.
Garter Stitch & Trinity Stitch—
Rows 1-4: Mauve—Knit across.
Row 5: Blue—Knit across.
Row 6: Knit 1, *Knit/Purl/Knit into one st, Purl 3 tog*. Rep *—* 15/16/17/18 more times. Knit/Purl/Knit into one st, Knit 1.
Row 7: Purl across.
Row 8: Knit 1, *Purl 3 tog, Knit/Purl/Knit into one st*. Rep *—* 15/16/17/18 more times. Purl 3 tog, Knit 1.
Rep rows 1-8, plus rows 1-5.
Trinity Stitch—
Row 1: Same as row 6.
Row 2: Purl across.
Row 3: Same as row 8.
Row 4: Purl across.
Continue working rows 1-4 until sleeve length is 15/16/17/18 in. (38/40.5/43/45.5 cm), or work to desired length.
Stockinette Stitch & Garter Stitch—
Row 1: Gray—Purl across.
Row 2: Knit across.

Rows 3, 4: Mauve—Knit across.
Row 5: Purl across.
Row 6: Gray—Knit and Dec 34 sts evenly across (33/37/41/45 sts remain).
Cuffs: Change to size 4 needles. Work Uneven Rib for 3½ in. (9 cm). From wrong side, Bind Off in Ribbing.

BLOCKING & PRESSING:
See pg. 120.

SEAM JOININGS: See pg. 121.

FRONT BAND: With Gray and from right side, Pick Up 257/265/273/281 sts (incl. 43 sts from safety pin). Place on circular needle and work Single Rib as on straight needles for 3 rows.
Buttonholes (right side): **Row 4**—Work Single Rib for 8 sts, *Bind Off 3, Single Rib for 7 sts*. Rep *—* 5 more times. Bind off 3. Continue working Single Rib.
Row 5: Work Single Rib and Inc 3 sts over every buttonhole.
Work 2 more rows. Bind Off in Ribbing.

FINISHING: Attach buttons to left Front band.

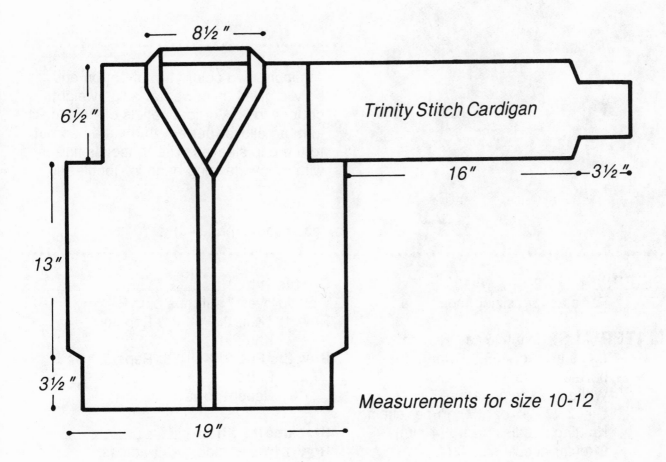

8½ "

6½ "

13"

3½ "

19"

Trinity Stitch Cardigan

16"

3½ "

Measurements for size 10-12

cap-sleeve top

A pebbly, two-color yarn of cotton and acrylic gives this sweater a lightweight, cottony look. Vertical panels of Double Rib form an allover pattern that is carried out to the cap sleeves. The V-neck is finished with an overlapping band in Double Rib.

(color photo, page 49)

SIZES: 8-10 / 12-14 / 16-18.
For standard sizing, see pg. 11.

MATERIALS: Chanteleine ''Rumba'' (54% acrylic, 46% cotton), imported by Merino Wool. Green-White (two-color yarn)—7/8/9 skeins @ 1¾ oz. (50 gr) per skein. Knitting needles size 6 (4 mm). Circular needle size 6 (4 mm).

GAUGE: Stockinette Stitch, 24 stitches and 32 rows = 4 in. (10 cm) square.

STITCHES USED: For abbreviations, see pg. 15. For how to knit, see pg. 108.

Double Rib_____
Worked over 4 stitches plus 2.
Row 1: *Knit 2, Purl 2*. Repeat *—*. Knit 2.
Row 2: *Purl 2, Knit 2*. Repeat *—*. Purl 2.
Repeat rows 1, 2.

Stockinette Stitch_____
Row 1 (wrong side): Knit across.
Row 2: Purl across.
Repeat rows 1, 2.

BACK: Cast On 106/114/126 sts.
Double Rib—
Row 1: *Knit 2, Purl 2*. Rep *—* 25/27/30 more times. Knit 2.
Row 2: *Purl 2, Knit 2*. Rep *—*. Purl 2.
Rep rows 1, 2 four more times.
Stockinette Stitch—
Row 11 (right side): Purl across.

Row 12: Knit across.

Rep rows 1, 2.

Work rows 1-14 five more times, or work to desired length.

Armholes (right side): **Row 1**—Bind Off 7 sts. Work pattern 92/100/112 sts (incl. bind off st). Bind Off remaining 7 sts. Cut yarn. Attach yarn and start next row. Continue working rows 1-14 three times. Work Stockinette Stitch until armhole length is 6½/7/7½ in. (16.5/18/19 cm).

Shoulders & Neck: From wrong side, Bind Off in Knit.

FRONT: Work same as Back as far as 4 repeats, plus rows 1-13.

Neck (wrong side): **Row 14**—Knit 50/54/60. Bind Off 6 sts. Knit 50/54/60 (incl. bind off st).

Note: Work each side separately (by placing left side on a separate needle), or work both sides together by using a second skein of yarn (attach at left neck opening). Dec 1 st every third row on Front edge until 22/24/26 sts remain.

Armholes: Work same as Back.

Shoulders: From wrong side, Bind Off in Knit 22/24/26 sts.

SHOULDER JOININGS: See pg. 121.

SLEEVES: From right side, Pick Up 78/86/90 sts (39/43/45 sts on each side of shoulder seam).

Stockinette Stitch—

Row 1 (wrong side): Knit across.

Row 2: Purl across.

Rep rows 1, 2.

Double Rib—

Row 5: *Knit 2, Purl 2*. Rep *—* 18/20/21 more times. Knit 2.

Row 6: *Purl 2, Knit 2*. Rep *—* 18/20/21 more times. Purl 2.

Rep rows 5, 6 four more times.

Rep rows 1-14, or work to desired length.

From right side, Bind Off in Ribbing.

BLOCKING & PRESSING:
See pg. 120.

SEAM JOININGS: See pg. 121.

NECKBAND: From right side, Pick Up 128/126/144 sts. Place on circular needle and work Double Rib as on straight needles for 1¼ in. (3 cm). From right side, Bind Off in Chain Knit.

NECK FINISHING (wrong side): Overlap front edges of neckband and attach to center opening.

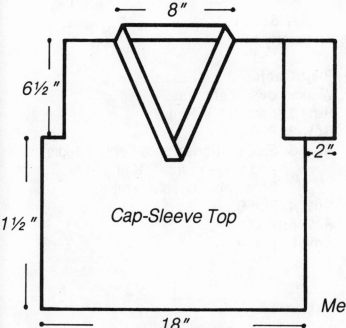

Cap-Sleeve Top

8"

6½"

2"

1½"

18"

Measurements for size 8-10

chenille jacket

This chenille, in the warmest of browns, takes on a furry look. A pattern of blocks and panels is formed in Stockinette Stitch. Cables are worked on the shoulders and on the full, gathered sleeves. The modified mandarin collar adds to the tailored style.

(color photo, page 89)

SIZES: 6-8 / 10-12 / 14-16
For standard sizing, see pg. 11.

MATERIALS: Chenille (100% cotton).
Brown—2 lb./2lb. 4 oz./2 lb. 8 oz.
(905/1020/1135 gr).
Knitting needles size 10 (6 mm).
Crochet hook size G (4.5 mm).

GAUGE: Pattern stitch, 12 stitches and
18 rows = 4 in. (10 cm) square.

STITCHES USED: For abbreviations,
see pg. 15. For how to knit, see
pg. 108.

Stockinette Stitch_____
Row 1 (right side): Knit across.
Row 2: Purl across.
Repeat rows 1, 2.

Reversed Stockinette Stitch_____
Row 1 (right side): Purl across.
Row 2: Knit across.
Repeat rows 1, 2.

Garter Stitch_____
Knit every row.

Plait Cable_____
Worked over 9 stitches.
Row 1 (right side): Knit 9.
Row 2: Purl 9.
Row 3: Slip 3 stitches onto cable needle
and leave in front, Knit 3, Knit 3
from cable needle, Knit 3.
Row 4: Purl 9.
Row 5: Knit 9.
Row 6: Purl 9.

Row 7: Knit 3, Slip 3 stitches onto cable needle and leave in back, Knit 3, Knit 3 from cable needle.
Row 8: Purl 9.
Repeat rows 1-8.

BACK: Cast On 57/64/68 sts.
Stockinette Stitch—
Row 1 (wrong side): Knit 1 (edge st), Purl 55/62/66, Knit 1 (edge st).
Row 2: Knit across.
Row 3: Knit 1, Purl, Knit 1.
Block & Panel Pattern—
Row 1 (right side): Knit 2/2/4, *Purl 4, Knit 3*. Rep *—* 6/7/7 more times. Purl 4, Knit 2/2/4.
Row 2: Knit 1, Purl 1/1/3, *Knit 4, Purl 3*. Rep *—* 6/7/7 more times. Knit 4, Purl 1/1/3, Knit 1.
Rep rows 1, 2 two more times.
Row 7: Knit across.
Row 8: Knit 1, Purl, Knit 1.
Row 9: Knit across.
Row 10 (wrong side): Same as row 2.
Row 11: Same as row 1.
Rep rows 10, 11 two more times.
Row 16: Knit 1, Purl, Knit 1.
Row 17: Knit across.
Row 18: Knit 1, Purl, Knit 1.
Rep rows 1-18 two more times, or work to desired length.
Block & Panel & Cable Pattern—
Row 1 (right side): Knit 1, Purl 19/19/21, *Knit 3, Purl 4*. Rep *—* 1/2/2 more times. Knit 3, Purl 19/19/21, Knit 1.
Row 2: Knit 20/20/22, *Purl 3, Knit 4*. Rep *—* 1/2/2 more times. Purl 3, Knit 20/20/22.
Rep rows 1, 2 two more times.
Row 7: Cable rows 1 and 5—Knit 1, Purl 7/7/9, Knit 1, Inc 1 (by picking up a st), Knit 2, Inc 1, Knit 2, Inc 1, Knit 1, Purl 6, Knit across 17/24/24, Purl 6, Knit 1, Inc 1, Knit 2, Inc 1, Knit 2, Inc 1, Knit 1, Purl 7/7/9, Knit 1.
Row 8: Knit 8/8/10, Purl 9, Knit 6, Purl across 17/24/24, Knit 6, Purl 9, Knit 8/8/10.
Armholes (right side): **Row 9**—Bind Off in Purl 6 sts. Purl 2/2/4 (incl. bind off st). Cable—row 3 (see stitch instructions). Purl 6, Knit across 17/24/24, Purl 6. Cable—row 7 (see stitch instructions). Purl 2/2/4. Bind Off remaining 6 sts. Cut yarn. Attach yarn and start next row.
Continue working Block & Panel & Cable Pattern until armhole length is 7½/7½/8 in. (19/19/20 cm). End by working Cable row 3 or 7.
Shoulders (wrong side): Bind Off in Knit 14/14/15 sts. Work pattern for 23/30/32 sts (incl. bind off st). Bind Off remaining 14/14/15 sts. Cut yarn.
Collar: Work pattern for 7 more rows. From wrong side, Bind Off in Chain Knit.

RIGHT FRONT: Cast On 29/32/34 sts.
Stockinette Stitch—
Row 1 (wrong side): Knit 1 (edge st), Purl 27/30/32, Knit 1 (edge st).
Row 2: Knit across.
Row 3: Knit 1, Purl, Knit 1.
Block & Panel Pattern—
Row 1 (right side): Knit 2/5/5, *Purl 4, Knit 3*. Rep *—* 2 more times. Purl 4, Knit 2/2/4.
Row 2: Knit 1, Purl 1/1/3, *Knit 4, Purl 3*. Rep *—* 2 more times. Knit 4, Purl 1/4/4, Knit 1.
Rep rows 1, 2 two more times.
Rows 7-9: Same as Back.
Row 10 (wrong side): Same as row 2.
Row 11: Same as row 1.
Rep rows 10, 11 two more times.
Rows 16-18: Same as Back.
Rep rows 1-18 two more times, or work to match Back.
Block & Panel & Cable Pattern—
Row 1 (right side): Knit 2/5/5, Purl 4, Knit 3, Purl 19/19/21, Knit 1.
Row 2: Knit 20/20/22, Purl 3, Knit 4, Purl 1/4/4, Knit 1.
Rep rows 1, 2 two more times.
Row 7: Cable row 5—Knit across 9/12/12. Purl 6, Knit 1, Inc 1, Knit 2, Inc 1, Knit 2, Inc 1, Knit 1, Purl 7/7/9, Knit 1.
Row 8: Knit 8/8/10, Purl 9, Knit 6, Purl across 8/11/11, Knit 1.

Armhole (right side): **Row 9**—Knit across 9/12/12, Purl 6. Cable—row 7 (see stitch instructions). Purl 2/2/4. Bind Off remaining 6 stitches. Cut yarn. Attach yarn and start next row.
Continue working Block & Panel & Cable Pattern same as Back.
Shoulders (wrong side): Bind Off in Knit 14/14/15 sts. Work pattern for 11/14/15 sts (incl. bind off st), Knit 1.
Collar: Work same as Back.

LEFT FRONT: Work same as right Front, but in reverse.
Armhole (right side): **Row 9**—Bind Off 6 sts. Purl 2/2/4 (incl. bind off st). Cable—row 3, Purl 6, Knit across 9/12/12.

SHOULDER JOININGS: See pg. 121.

SLEEVES: From wrong side, Pick Up 47/47/51 sts (23/23/25 sts from each side, plus 1 st from shoulder seam).

Reversed Stockinette Stitch & Cable Pattern—
Row 1 (right side): Knit 1, Purl 18/18/20, Cable—row 7 for right sleeve, row 3 for left sleeve. Purl 18/18/20, Knit 1.
Row 2: Knit 19/19/21, Purl 9, Knit 19/19/21.
Continue working pattern until sleeve length is 17½/18¼/18¾ in. (44.5/46.5/47.5 cm), or work to desired length. End by working Cable row 3 or 7.
Row 4 or 8: Knit across.
Cuffs: Purl 2 tog across row. Work 7 rows of Reversed Stockinette Stitch. From right side, Bind Off in Purl.

BLOCKING & PRESSING:
See pg. 120.

SEAM JOININGS: See pg. 121.

FINISHING (right side): Work Single Crochet across bottom edge (see A and B under Reversed Single Crochet, pg. 123.)

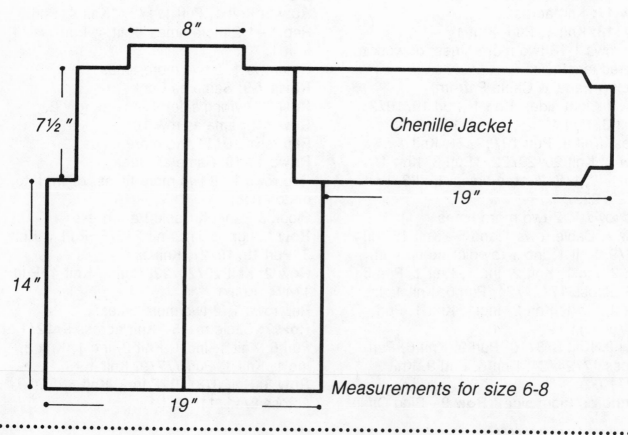

Chenille Jacket

8"

7½"

14"

19"

19"

Measurements for size 6-8

88

Chenille Jacket, page 86

Silk Tunic, page 62

90 *Lattice Lace Pullover, page 97*   *Gray & White Top, page 100*

Puffed-Sleeve Top, page 102   *Golden Top, page 104*   91

mauve alpaca cardigan

It's the silkiest of yarns in the softest of colors. Luxurious alpaca is worked in lacy ribs that run vertically between panels of Crossed Stockinette Stitch. Trinity Stitch clusters cap the shoulders for natural padding.

SIZES: 6-8 / 10-12 / 14-16
For standard sizing, see pg. 11.

MATERIALS: Georges Picaud ''Alpaga'' (100% alpaca), imported by Merino Wool. Mauve—9/10/11 skeins @ 1¾ oz. (50 gr) per skein. Knitting needles size 7 (4.5 mm). 16 buttons.

GAUGE: Crossed Stockinette Stitch with 2 strands, 20 stitches and 24 rows = 4 in. (10 cm) square.

STITCHES USED: For abbreviations, see pg. 15. For how to knit, see pg. 108.

Double Twist Rib_____
Worked over 4 stitches plus 2.
Row 1 (wrong side): *Purl 2, Twist Knit 2*. Repeat *—*. Purl 2.
Row 2: *Twist Knit 2, Purl 2*. Repeat *—*. Twist Knit 2.
Repeat rows 1, 2.

Crossed Stockinette Stitch_____
Row 1 (right side): Twist Knit across.
Row 2: Purl across.
Repeat rows 1, 2.

Lace Stitch_____
Worked over 5 stitches.
Row 1 (right side): Purl 2 together, Yo, Knit 1, Yo, Purl 2 together.
Row 2: Purl across.
Repeat rows 1, 2.

Trinity Stitch_____
Worked over 4 stitches plus 2.
Row 1 (wrong side): Knit 1, *Knit 1/Purl 1/Knit 1 into one stitch, Purl 3 together*. Repeat *—*. Knit 1.
Row 2: Purl across.
Row 3: Knit 1, *Purl 3 together, Knit 1/Purl 1/Knit 1 into one stitch*. Repeat *—*. Knit 1.
Row 4: Purl across.
Repeat rows 1-4.

_____
Note: Work with two strands of yarn throughout.
Note: Edge stitches are not included in stitch instructions, above. See edge stitches, pg. 116.

BACK: Cast On 78/82/94 sts and work Double Twist Rib for 3 in. (7.5 cm). Crossed Stockinette Stitch—
Row 1 (right side): Twist Knit across and Inc 7/8/6 sts. Inc 1 st on each side edge, remaining 5/6/4 sts evenly across (85/90/100 sts).
Row 2: Knit 1, Purl 83/88/98, Knit 1. Pattern—
Row 1 (right side): Knit 1 (edge st), Twist Knit 11/13/13, *Purl 4/4/5, Purl 2 tog, Yo, Knit 1, Yo, Purl 2 tog*. Rep *—* 2 more times. Purl 7/8/12, *Purl 2 tog, Yo, Knit 1, Yo, Purl 2 tog, Purl 4/4/5*. Rep *—* 2 more times. Twist Knit 11/13/13, Knit 1 (edge st).
Row 2: Knit 1, Purl 11/13/13, *Twist Knit 4/4/5, Purl 5*. Rep *—* 2 more times. Twist Knit 7/8/12, *Purl 5, Twist Knit 4/4/5*. Rep *—* 2 more times. Purl 11/13/13, Knit 1.
Rep rows 1, 2 for 10½ in. (26 cm), or work to desired length.
Armholes: From right side, Bind Off in Knit 11/13/13 sts. Work pattern 63/64/74 sts (incl. bind off st). Bind Off remaining 11/13/13 sts. Cut yarns. Attach yarns and start next row.
Row 1 (wrong side): Knit 1, *Twist Knit 4/4/5, Purl 5*. Rep *—* two more times. Twist Knit 7/8/12, *Purl 5, Twist Knit 4/4/5*. Rep *—* 2 more times. Knit 1.
Continue to work pattern for 5½/6/6½ in. (14/15/16.5 cm).
Neck (right side): Work 14/14/16 sts. Bind Off in Purl 35/36/42 sts. Work remaining 14/14/16 sts (incl. bind off st).
Shoulders (both stay on needle, but are worked separately): Work pattern 3 more rows. From right side, Bind Off in Purl.

RIGHT FRONT: Cast On 46/46/50 sts.
Row 1 (wrong side): *Purl 2, Twist Knit 2*. Rep *—* 9/9/10 more times. Purl 5, Knit 1 (edge st).
Row 2: Knit 1, Twist Knit 5, *Purl 2, Knit 2*. Rep *—* 9/9/10 more times.
Row 3: Same as row 1 except for last 6 sts. Purl 1, Purl 2 tog, Yo, Purl 2, Knit 1 (buttonhole).
Row 4: Same as row 2.
Rep rows 1, 2 two more times, plus rows 3, 4. Work Double Twist Rib for 3 in. (7.5 cm).
Note: Work Front band the same throughout, making a buttonhole every 6th row for a total of 16 buttonholes.
Crossed Stockinette Stitch—
Row 1 (right side): Knit 1, Twist Knit across and Inc 1/3/4 sts. Inc 1 st on right side edge, remaining 0/2/3 sts evenly in pattern area (47/49/54 sts).
Row 2: Knit 1, Purl 45/47/52, Knit 1. Pattern—
Row 1 (right side): Knit 1, Twist Knit 5, Purl 2/2/4, *Purl 2 tog, Yo, Knit 1, Yo, Purl 2 tog, Purl 4/4/5*. Rep *—* 2 more times. Twist Knit 11/13/13, Knit 1.
Row 2: Knit 1, Purl 11/13/13, *Twist Knit 4/4/5, Purl 5*. Rep *—* 2 more times. Twist Knit 2/2/4, Purl 5, Knit 1.
Rep rows 1, 2 for 10½ in. (26 cm).
Armhole (right side): Work pattern for 34/36/41 sts. Bind Off in Knit remaining 13 sts. Cut yarns. Attach yarns and start next row.
Continue to work pattern for 4/4½/5 in. (10/11.5/13 cm).
Neck (right side): Place Front band 6 sts on a safety pin. Bind Off in Purl 16/16/19 sts. Work pattern, Knit 1.
Shoulder: Work pattern for 2 in. (5 cm). From right side, Bind Off in Purl.

LEFT FRONT: Work same as right Front, but in reverse, omitting buttonholes.

SHOULDER JOININGS: See pg. 121.

SLEEVES: From wrong side, Pick Up 71/75/81 sts (35/37/40 sts on each side, plus 1 st from shoulder seam).
Row 1 (right side): Knit across.
Note: Working Knit into front of stitch will give a twist effect to Pick Up stitch.
Trinity Stitch—
Row 1: Knit 1 (edge st), Twist Knit 2/2/1, *Knit/Purl/Knit into one stitch, Purl 3 tog*. Rep *—* 15/16/18 more times. Knit/Purl/Knit into one stitch, Twist Knit 2/2/1, Knit 1 (edge st).
Row 2: Knit 1, Purl, Knit 1.
Row 3: Knit 1, Twist Knit 2/2/1, *Purl 3 tog, Knit/Purl/Knit into one stitch*. Rep *—* 15/16/18 more times. Purl 3 tog, Twist Knit 2/2/1, Knit 1.
Row 4: Knit 1, Purl, Knit 1.
Rep rows 1-4 for 2½ in. (6 cm).
Note: On last row (row 4) of Trinity Stitch, instead of working Purl, work Twist Knit across.
Row 5: Knit 1, Purl across and Dec evenly 10 sts, Knit 1 (61/65/71 sts).
Pattern—
Row 1 (right side): Knit 1, Purl 3/2/2, *Purl 2 tog, Yo, Knit 1, Yo, Purl 2 tog, Purl 3/4/5*. Rep *—* 5 more times. Purl 2 tog, Yo, Knit 1, Yo, Purl 2 tog, Purl 3/2/2, Knit 1.
Row 2: Knit 1, Twist Knit 3/2/2, *Purl 5, Twist Knit 3/4/5*. Rep *—* 5 more times. Purl 5, Twist Knit 3/2/2, Knit 1.
Rep rows 1, 2 for 14½/15/15 in. (37/38/38 cm).

Crossed Stockinette Stitch—
Row 1 (right side): Knit 1, Twist Knit 59/63/69, Knit 1.
Row 2: Knit 1, Purl across and Dec evenly 23/23/25 sts. Knit 1.
Cuffs: Row 1—Twist Knit 2, *Purl 2, Twist Knit 2*. Rep *—* 8/9/10 more times.
Row 2: Purl 2, *Twist Knit 2, Purl 2*. Rep *—* 8/9/10 more times.
Rep rows 1, 2 for 3 in. (7.5 cm). From wrong side, Bind Off in Ribbing.

NECKBAND: Place the 6 sts of right Front band on needle. From right side, Pick Up 74/76/86 sts around neck. Place remaining 6 sts of left Front band on second needle and Twist Knit 5, Knit 1 onto right-hand needle (86/88/98).
Row 1 (wrong side): Knit 1, Purl 5, Twist Knit 2/3/2, Purl 2, *Twist Knit 2, Purl 2*. Rep *—* 16/16/19 more times. Twist Knit 2/3/2, Purl 5, Knit 1.
Row 2: Knit 1, Twist Knit 5, Purl 2/3/2, Twist Knit 2, *Purl 2, Twist Knit 2*. Rep *—* 16/16/19 more times. Purl 2/3/2, Twist Knit 5, Knit 1.
Rep rows 1, 2 four more times. From wrong side, Bind Off the first 6 sts in Knit, Double Twist Rib in Ribbing, and remaining 6 sts in Knit.

BLOCKING & PRESSING:
See pg. 120.

SEAM JOININGS: See pg. 121.

FINISHING: Attach buttons to left Front band.   ▷

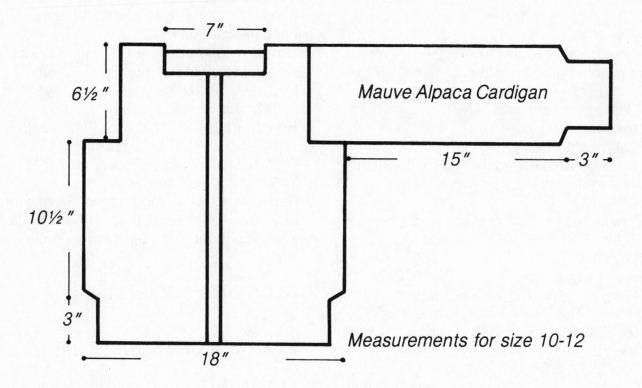

7"

6½"

Mauve Alpaca Cardigan

10½"

15"   3"

3"

18"

Measurements for size 10-12

lattice lace pullover

A wool-blend yarn is worked in an overall Lattice Lace Stitch to create the illusion of double-knit thickness. The gently squared neckline and gracefully gathered sleeves add to the softness.

(color photo, page 90)

SIZES: 6-8 / 10-12 / 14-16 / 18
For standard sizing, see pg. 11.

MATERIALS: Pingouin ''Confortable'' (55% wool, 45% acrylic). Ecru— 8/8/9/9 skeins @ 1¾ oz. (50 gr) per skein.
Knitting needles size 6 (4 mm) and size 8 (5 mm).
Crochet hook size F (4 mm).

GAUGE: Lattice Lace Stitch and size 8 needles, 20 stitches = 4 in. (10 cm).

STITCHES USED: For abbreviations, see pg. 15. For how to knit, see pg. 108.

Twist Rib_____
Worked over 3 stitches plus 2.
Row 1 (wrong side): *Purl 2, Twist Knit 1*. Repeat *—*. Purl 2.
Row 2: *Twist Knit 2, Purl 1*. Repeat *—*. Twist Knit 2.
Repeat rows 1, 2.

Lattice Lace Stitch_____
Worked over 3 stitches plus 1.
Row 1 (right side): *Slip 1, Knit 2, Psso, Yo*. Repeat *—*. Knit 1.
Row 2: Purl across.
Row 3: Knit 1, *Yo, Slip 1, Knit 2, Psso*. Repeat *—*. ▷

Row 4: Purl across.
   Repeat rows 1-4.
Note: All Slip Stitches are slipped purlwise with yarn in back.

Note: Edge stitches are not included in stitch instructions, above. See edge stitches, pg. 116.

BACK: With size 6 needles, Cast On 83/86/98/104 sts and work Twist Rib for 2½ in. (6.5 cm).
Stockinette Stitch—Change to size 8 needles.
Row 1 (right side): Knit across and Inc 7 sts. Inc 1 st on each edge, remaining 5 sts evenly across.
Row 2: Knit 1 (edge st), Purl 88/91/103/109, Knit 1 (edge st).
Lattice Lace Pattern—
Row 1 (right side): Knit 1, *Slip 1, Knit 2, Psso, Yo*. Rep *—* 28/29/33/35 more times. Knit 2.
Row 2: Knit 1, Purl 88/91/103/109, Knit 1.
Row 3: Knit 2, *Yo, Slip 1, Knit 2, Psso*. Rep *—* 28/29/33/35 more times. Knit 1.
Row 4: Same as row 2.
Rep rows 1-4 for 12 in. (30 cm), or work to desired length.
Armholes (right side): **Row 1**—Bind Off in Chain Knit 12 sts. Work pattern 66/69/81/87 sts (incl. bind off st). Bind Off remaining 12 sts. Cut yarn. Attach yarn and start next row.
Continue working for 5½/6/6½/7 in. (14/15/16.5/18 cm).
Neck (right side): **Row 1**—Work pattern 21/21/24/27 sts. Bind Off in Chain Knit 24/27/33/33 sts. Work remaining 21/21/24/27 sts (incl. bind off st).
Shoulders (both stay on needle, but are worked separately): Work pattern 3 more rows. From right side, Bind Off in Chain Knit.

FRONT: Work same as Back as far as armhole, plus 1½/2/2½/3 in. (4/5/6.5/7.5 cm).
Neck (right side): Work same as Back. Work each side separately by placing left side on a safety pin. Work pattern for 4½ in. (11.5 cm), or work to match Back.
Shoulders: From right side, Bind Off in Chain Knit.
Left side: Work same as right side.

SHOULDER JOININGS: See pg. 121.

SLEEVES: From right side and on size 8 needle, Pick Up 60/66/72/78 sts (30/33/36/39 sts on each side of shoulder seam).
Row 1 (wrong side): Knit 1 (edge st), Purl 58/64/70/76 sts, Knit 1 (edge st).
Lattice Lace Pattern—
Continue to work pattern rows 1-4 until sleeve length is 16/17/17½/17¾ in. (40.5/43/44.5/45 cm), or work to desired length.
Stockinette Stitch—
Row 1 (right side): Knit across.
Row 2: Purl and Dec 25/26/25/25 sts evenly across.
Cuffs: Change to size 6 needles. Work Twist Rib for 2 in. (5 cm). From right side, Bind Off in Ribbing.

BLOCKING & PRESSING:
See pg. 120.

SEAM JOININGS: See pg. 121.

NECK FINISHING: Reversed Single Crochet. See pg. 123.

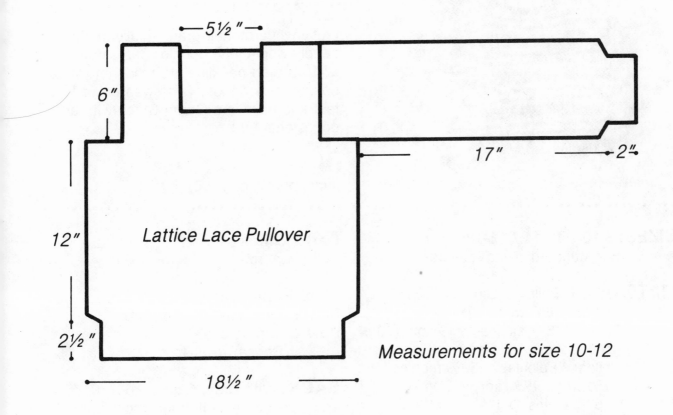

Lattice Lace Pullover

5½"

6"

12"

2½"

18½"

17"

2"

Measurements for size 10-12

gray & white top

Fluffy white mohair dramatically frosts a pebbly wool-blend bouclé. Cap-sleeve cuffs and squared neckline are rolled into wide, double-thick bands. This sweater works up fast and easy in a Garter Stitch with an occasional Purl.

(color photo, page 90)

SIZES: 8-10 / 12-14 / 16-18
For standard sizing, see pg. 11.

MATERIALS: Phildar ''Gin-Fizz'' (37% mohair, 36% wool, 27% acrylic). Gray—6/6/7 skeins @ 1¾ oz. (50 gr) per skein.
Phildar ''Falbalas'' (50% mohair, 31% wool, 19% acrylic). White—5/5/6 skeins @ 1²/₅ oz. (40 gr) per skein.
Knitting needles size 10 (6 mm).
Circular needle size 10 (6 mm).

GAUGE: Stockinette Stitch, 10 stitches = 3 in. (7.5 cm).

STITCHES USED: For abbreviations, see pg. 15. For how to knit, see pg. 108.

Garter Stitch_____
Knit every row.

Stockinette Stitch_____
Row 1 (right side): Knit across.
Row 2: Purl across.
           Repeat rows 1, 2.

BACK: With Gray, Cast On 64/70/76 sts and work Garter Stitch for 6 rows, plus 1 row Purl.
Note: First row is wrong side.
Row 1 (right side): White—Knit across.
Row 2: Knit across.
Rows 3, 4: Gray—Knit across.
Rows 5, 6: White—Knit across.
Rows 7, 8: Gray—Knit across.
Rows 9, 10: White—Knit across.
Row 11 (right side): Gray—Knit across.
Row 12: Purl across.
Rows 13-15: Knit across.

Row 16: Purl across.
Rep rows 1-16 two more times, plus rows 1-15. Knitting measures 12½ in. (32 cm). Or work to desired length.
Armholes (wrong side): **Row 16**—Bind Off in Purl 9 sts. Purl 46/52/58 (incl. bind off st). Bind Off remaining 9 sts. Cut yarn. Attach yarn and start next row. Continue working rows 1-16 twice, plus rows 1-10.
Shoulder Panel: Work 5/7/9 rows of White in Garter Stitch. Armhole length is 7¾/8/8¼ in. (19.5/20.5/21 cm). From wrong side, Bind Off in Knit.

FRONT: Work same as Back as far as armholes.
Armholes & Neck: Row 16—Bind Off in Purl 9 sts. Purl 12/14/16 (incl. bind off st). Bind Off 22/24/26 sts. Purl 12/14/16 (incl. bind off st). Bind Off remaining 9 sts. Cut yarn. Attach yarn and start next row. Work each side separately by placing left side on a safety pin. Continue working rows 1-16 twice, plus rows 1-10, plus shoulder panel (see Back).
Left side: Work same as right side.

SHOULDER JOININGS: See pg. 121.

SLEEVES: With Gray and from right side, Pick Up 51/53/55 sts (25/26/27 sts on each side, plus 1 st from shoulder seam).
Rows 1-18: Work Garter Stitch.
Row 19: Purl across.

Rows 20, 2l: White—Knit across.
Rows 22, 23: Gray—Knit across.
Rows 24, 25: White—Knit across.
Rows 26, 27: Gray—Knit across.
Rows 28-41: White—Knit across.
From right side, Bind Off in Knit.

BLOCKING & PRESSING:
See pg. 120.

SEAM JOININGS: See pg. 121.

COLLAR: With Gray and from wrong side at shoulder seam, Pick Up 100/112/116 sts. Place on circular needle.
Row 1: Knit one round.
Row 2: White—Purl one round.
Row 3: Knit one round.
Rep rows 2, 3 seven more times, plus row 2.
From right side, Bind Off in Knit.

NECK & SLEEVE FINISHING
(right side): Fold collar in half and carefully attach bind off edge to "pick up yarn" on right side.
Attach bind off edge on sleeve to first row of white.

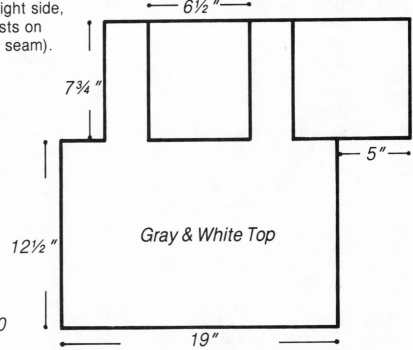

Gray & White Top

— 6½ " —

7¾ "

5 "

12½ "

Measurements for size 8-10

19 "

puffed-sleeve top

Mohair in a soft multi-rose color forms Garter Stitch ridges on the body of this Lattice Lace Stitch sweater. The short puffy mohair sleeves, also worked in Garter Stitch, are gathered for more fullness.

(color photo, page 91)

SIZES: 8-10 / 12-14 / 16-18
For standard sizing, see pg. 11.

MATERIALS: Phildar "Discretion" (70% acrylic, 30% wool). Mauve—5/5/6 skeins @ 1¾ oz. (50 gr) per skein. Phildar "Beaugency" (50% mohair, 31% wool, 19% acrylic). Rose—3/3/4 skeins @ 1²/₅ oz. (40 gr) per skein.
Knitting needles size 6 (4 mm), size 7 (4.5 mm) and size 10 (6 mm).

GAUGE: Lattice Lace Stitch and size 7 needles, 24 stitches = 4 in. (10 cm).

STITCHES USED: For abbreviations, see pg. 15. For how to knit, see pg. 108.

Stockinette Stitch_____
Row 1 (right side): Knit across.

Row 2: Purl across.
Repeat rows 1, 2.

Garter Stitch_____
Knit every row.

Lattice Lace Stitch_____
Worked over 3 stitches plus 1.
Row 1 (right side): *Slip 1, Knit 2, Psso, Yo*. Repeat *—*. Knit 1.
Row 2: Purl across.
Row 3: Knit 1, *Yo, Slip 1, Knit 2, Psso*. Repeat *—*.
Row 4: Purl across.
Repeat rows 1-4.
Note: All Slip Stitches are slipped purlwise with yarn in back.

_____
Note: Edge stitches are not included in stitch instructions, above. See edge stitches, pg. 116.

BACK: With Mauve and size 6 needles, Cast On 99/108/117 sts and work hem.
Stockinette Stitch—
Row 1 (wrong side): Knit across.
Row 2: Knit 1 (edge st), Purl 97/106/115, Knit 1 (edge st).
Rep rows 1, 2 two more times.
Garter Stitch—
Rows 7, 8: Knit across. End of hem.
Stockinette Stitch—Change to size 7 needles.
Row 9: Knit 1, Purl 97/106/115, Knit 1.
Row 10: Knit across.
Row 11: Knit 1, Purl, Knit 1.
Garter Stitch Ridge—Change to size 6 needles.
Rows 1, 2: Mohair—Knit across.
Lattice Lace Stitch—Change to size 7 needles.
Row 3 (right side): Mauve—Knit across.
Row 4: Knit 1, Purl 97/106/115, Knit 1.
Row 5: Knit 1, *Slip 1, Knit 2, Psso, Yo*.
Rep *—* 31/34/37 more times, Knit 2.
Row 6: Knit 1, Purl, Knit 1.
Row 7: Knit 2, *Yo, Slip 1, Knit 2, Psso*.
Rep *—* 31/34/37 more times. Knit 1.
Row 8: Knit 1, Purl, Knit 1.
Rep rows 5-8 two more times.
Row 17: Knit across.
Row 18: Knit 1, Purl, Knit 1.
Rep Garter Stitch Ridge rows 1, 2 and Lattice Lace Stitch rows 3-18 four more times, plus rows 1-4. Or work to desired length, adding one or more complete repeats.

Armholes (right side): **Row 5**—Bind Off in Chain Knit 8 sts. Work pattern 83/92/101 sts (incl. bind off st). Bind Off remaining 8 sts. Cut yarn. Attach yarn and start next row. Continue to work rows 6-18.
Work rows 1-18 twice, plus rows 1, 2.
Continue working Stockinette Stitch until armhole length is 6½/7/7½ in. (16.5/18/19 cm).
Neck & Shoulders: From right side, Bind Off in Chain Knit.

FRONT: Work same as Back.

SHOULDER JOININGS: Whipstitch each shoulder for 2 in. (5 cm). See pg. 121.

SLEEVES: With Mohair and size 10 needle, from right side, Pick Up 56/58/60 sts (28/29/30 sts on each side of shoulder seam). Work Garter Stitch for 9 in. (23 cm), or work to desired length. Dec 18 sts evenly across, or decrease to fit upper arm. Work 1 more row. Bind Off in Chain Knit.

BLOCKING & PRESSING:
See pg. 120.

SEAM JOININGS: See pg. 121.

FINISHING: Fold hem and carefully attach to wrong side.

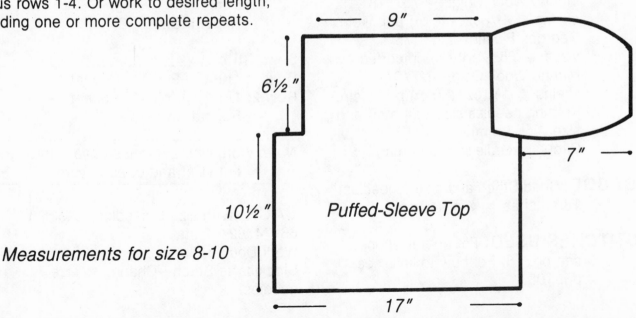

Measurements for size 8-10

Puffed-Sleeve Top

golden top

Natural-colored, twisted cotton combines with a silky gold-colored yarn to give this Seed Stitch sweater a pearly, shimmering sheen. The neck finish, worked all in gold, doubles over to form a delicate picot edge.

(color photo, page 91)

SIZES: 6-8 / 10-12 / 14-16 / 18
For standard sizing, see pg. 11.

MATERIALS: Georges Picaud ''Fric Frac'' (100% cotton), imported by Merino Wool. Beige—5/6/7/8 skeins @ 1²/₅ oz. (40 gr) per skein. Georges Picaud ''Zig'' (75% viscose, 25% cotton), imported by Merino Wool. Gold—6/7/8/9 skeins @ 1¾ oz. (50 gr) per skein. Knitting needles size 6 (4 mm) and size 7 (4.5 mm). Circular needle size 6 (4 mm).

GAUGE: Seed Stitch and size 7 needles, 18 stitches = 4 in. (10 cm).

STITCHES USED: For abbreviations, see pg. 15. For how to knit, see pg. 108.

Double Rib
Worked over 4 stitches plus 2.
Row 1 (wrong side): *Knit 2, Purl 2*. Repeat *—*. Knit 2.
Row 2: *Purl 2, Knit 2*. Repeat *—*. Purl 2.
Repeat rows 1, 2.

Seed Stitch
Row 1: *Knit 1, Purl 1*. Repeat *—*.
Row 2: *Purl 1, Knit 1*. Repeat *—*. Repeat rows 1, 2.

Note: Work with 2 strands of yarn throughout (1 strand of each yarn).

BACK: With size 6 needles, Cast On 66/74/82/90 sts.
Work Double Rib for 2½ in. (6.5 cm). Stockinette Stitch—Change to size 7 needles.

Row 1 (right side): Knit across and Inc 10/8/9/6 sts. Inc 1 st on each side edge, remaining 8/6/7/4 sts evenly across.
Row 2: Knit 1 (edge st), Purl 74/80/89/94, Knit 1 (edge st).
Seed Stitch—
Work Seed Stitch for 11½ in. (29 cm), or work to desired length.
Armholes: From right side, Bind Off in Chain Knit 12 sts. Work pattern 52/58/67/72 sts (incl. bind off st). Bind Off remaining 12 sts. Cut yarns. Attach yarns and start next row.
Continue to work pattern for 5½/6/6½/7 in. (14/15/16.5/18 cm).
Neck (right side): Work pattern 10/12/15/16 sts. Bind Off in Chain Knit 32/34/37/40 sts. Work remaining 10/12/15/16 sts (incl. bind off st).
Shoulders (both stay on needle, but are worked separately): Work pattern 3 more rows. From right side, Bind Off in Chain Knit.

FRONT: Work same as Back as far as armholes, plus 1/1½/2/2½ in. (2.5/4/5/6.5 cm).
Neck (right side): Work same as Back. Work each side separately by placing left side on a safety pin.
Continue working pattern until armhole length is 6/6½/7/7½ in. (15/16.5/18/19 cm), or work to match Back.
Shoulder: From right side, Bind Off in Chain Knit.
Left side: Work same as right side.

SHOULDER JOININGS: See pg. 121.

SLEEVES: From right side and on size 7 needle, Pick Up 69/74/79/84 sts (34/37/39/42 sts on each side plus 1/0/1/0 st from shoulder seam).
Work pattern for 6½ in. (16.5 cm), or work to desired length.
Stockinette Stitch—
Row 1 (right side): Knit across.
Row 2: Purl and Dec 15/16/13/14 sts evenly across.

Cuffs: Change to size 6 needles and work Double Rib for 1¾ in. (4.5 cm). From right side, Bind Off in Ribbing.

BLOCKING & PRESSING:
See pg. 120.

SEAM JOININGS: See pg. 121.

NECK FINISHING: With 2 strands of Gold and from wrong side, Pick Up an even number of sts (approx. 1 st in each Seed Stitch). Place on circular needle.
Row 1: Purl 1 round.
Rows 2-7: Knit 6 rounds.
Row 8 (Turn work around, as knitted on straight needles): *Purl 2 tog, Yo*.
Rep *—*.
Row 9 (Turn work around): Knit 1 round.
Rows 10-12: Knit 3 rounds.
From right side, Bind Off in Knit. Join edges.
Fold in half (Purl side in) over neckline and carefully attach outer edge of bind off stitch to ''pick up yarn.''

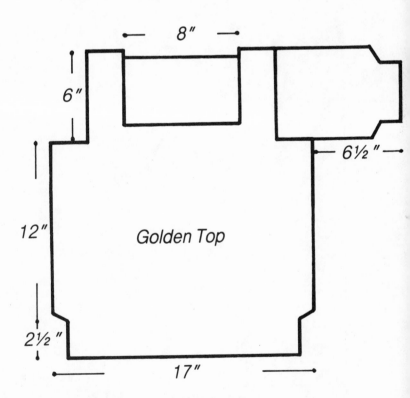

Measurements for size 6-8

Procedures

how to knit

CASTING ON: Cast On with two needles held closely together. The advantage of this method is that stitches can be placed firmly and evenly around needles. This also makes the first row easy to work and gives the stitches the same tension as the rest of the knitting.

Note: The length of yarn needed to Cast On depends on thickness of yarn and needles. As a rule, measure off 1¼ in. (3 cm) for each stitch to be Cast On, plus 5 in. (12.5 cm).

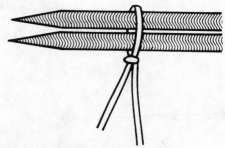

Step 2. Place the two needles through loop and pull knot tightly around needles (first stitch).

Step 1. Make a slip knot with yarn.

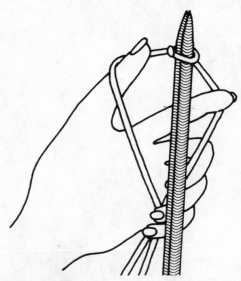

Step 3. Form a triangle with the yarn. The thumb holds free end of yarn, and the forefinger holds yarn from the ball.

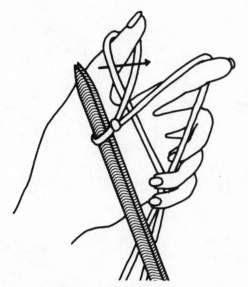

Step 4. Move needles carefully to the left of thumb, letting yarn strands slide evenly. Following arrow, move needles under yarn and up out of loop.

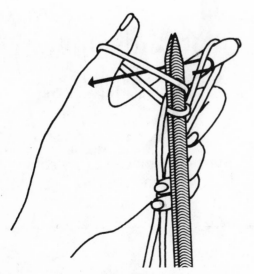

Step 5. Move needles toward forefinger. Following arrow, move needles under yarn and into loop.

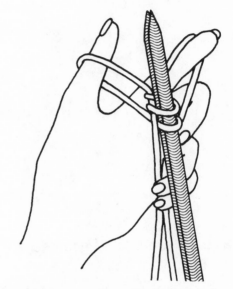

Step 6. Pull new stitch through.

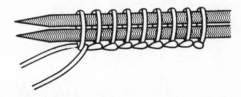

Step 7. Drop yarn from thumb and tighten stitch. Repeat steps 3-7 until required number of stitches are made. Place each new stitch next to previous stitch.

Step 8. Remove one of the needles carefully without dropping any stitches.

KNIT & PURL: The two basic stitches in knitting. Always work from right to left. The left hand holds the needle with unworked stitches and the right hand holds the needle with worked stitches.

Knit (Continental method; yarn is held in the left hand*)—

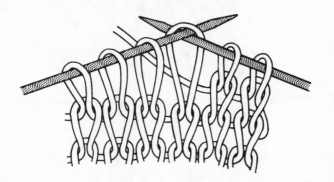

Step 1. Insert right-hand needle into stitch.

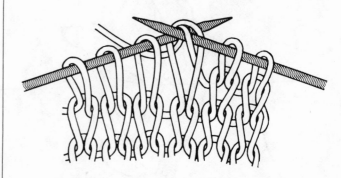

Step 3. Pull yarn through stitch to front.

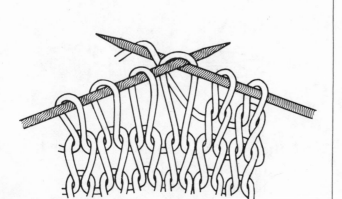

Step 2. Move the same needle behind and under yarn that is held over left forefinger.

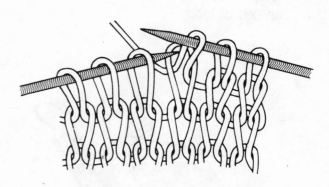

Step 4. Remove the old stitch from left-hand needle.

**Note:* In the English method, the yarn is held in the right hand, which takes it under and over the needle in Step 2.

Purl (Continental method*)—

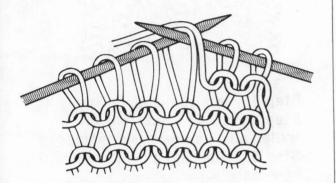

Step 1. Place yarn on front side and to the right of stitch. Insert right-hand needle under yarn and into stitch.

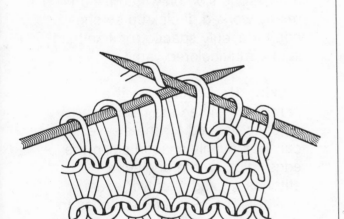

Step 2. Move needle behind and under yarn, as in Knit.

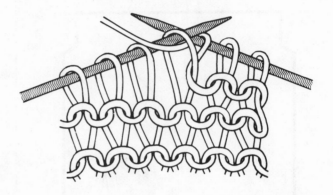

Step 3. Pull yarn through stitch to back.

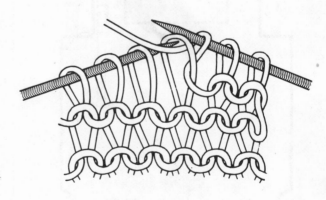

Step 4. Remove the old stitch from left-hand needle.

With practice, each set of Knit or Purl steps will become almost one. The left forefinger, which is "feeding" the yarn that is pulled through, will in time "learn" to give or to tighten the flow of yarn.

PICKING UP STITCHES:

From right or wrong side, pick up stitches along the edge of an armhole, neckline or front. Use a D or E (3-3.5 mm) crochet hook and work from right to left.

Note: Before starting, weave in all yarn ends (see pg. 123).

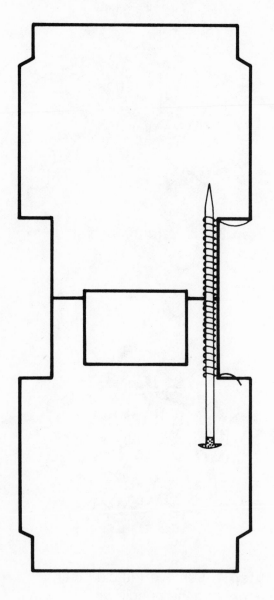

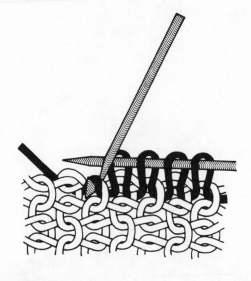

Step 1. Place yarn under edge.
Step 2. Pick up a loop through knitted stitch in row below edge.
Step 3. Place loop around right-hand needle.
Repeat steps 2, 3 until required number of stitches are picked up.

Picking up stitches from wrong side creates a decorative ridge on the right side. Pick up stitches from wrong side only if edges are neatly worked, if pick-up stitches can be evenly spaced, or if knitting is in a multicolored yarn.

Picking Up Stitches in the Armhole—When the number of stitches needed for the sleeve can't be evenly spaced along the edge, pick up the additional stitches around shoulder seam.

Note: The number of stitches to be picked up for a sleeve is based on armhole length and stitch gauge.

There are always more rows than stitches to the gauge. For example, instructions may call for 67 stitches to be picked up (33 stitches on each side of shoulder seam, plus 1 stitch from shoulder seam), and there are 36 "spaces" on each side. Begin by picking up 2 stitches, skip one space, pick up 2 stitches, skip one space, pick up 2 stitches, skip one space, then pick up remaining 27 stitches in the remaining 27 spaces. Pick up one stitch from the shoulder seam. Work the other side of the seam the same way, but in reverse.

A similar method is used when working a puffed sleeve. Start adding all the extra stitches halfway between first picked-up stitch and shoulder.

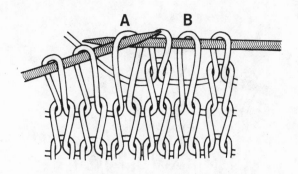

SLIP STITCH: Lift a stitch from left-hand needle onto right-hand needle without working it. If Slip Stitch is made from right side, yarn is carried behind the slipped stitch, as shown above.

A. Knitwise—Slip as if to Knit.

B. Purlwise—Slip as if to Purl.

If Slip Stitch is made from wrong side, yarn is carried in front of the slipped stitch.

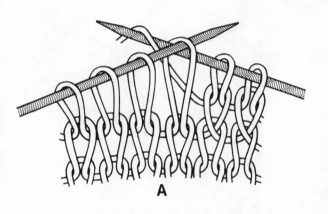

A

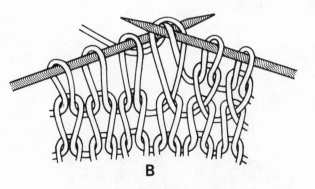

B

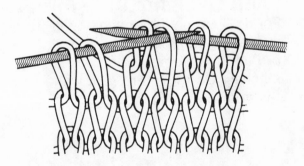

PASS SLIPPED STITCH OVER (Psso): With left-hand needle, lift slipped stitch over worked stitch or stitches.

TWIST KNIT: This is a variation of regular Knit. Work by inserting needle into back of stitch (A). Pull yarn through to front (B).

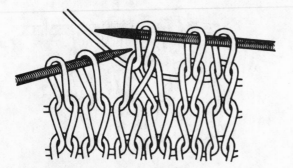

STITCHES WORKED TOGETHER (sts tog): Work two or more stitches together as one stitch, either in Knit or Purl.

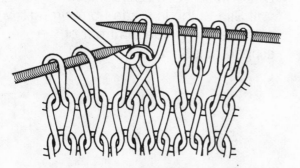

YARN OVER NEEDLE (Yo):
Form a loop on right-hand needle by placing yarn over needle. Knit or Purl the following stitch or stitches. On the return row, work "yarn over" stitch in Knit or Purl.

INCREASING (Inc): Shape by adding stitches.

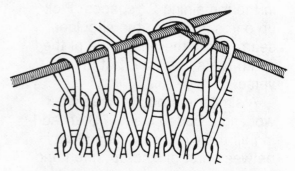

Step 1. Knit into front of stitch. Don't remove old stitch.

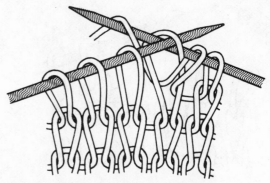

Step 2. Knit into back of same stitch, making a Twist Knit.

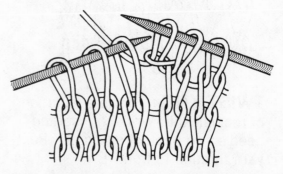

Step 3. Remove the old stitch from left-hand needle, leaving an extra stitch on right-hand needle.

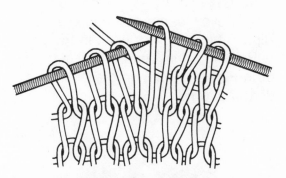

PICK UP A STITCH: Add an extra stitch by picking up a loop between two stitches from row below. Place new stitch on left-hand needle, and work either in Knit or Purl.

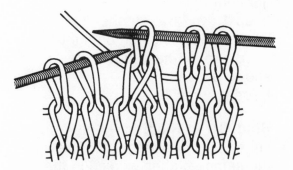

DECREASING (Dec): Shape by reducing stitches. Work two stitches together in intervals either in Knit or Purl.

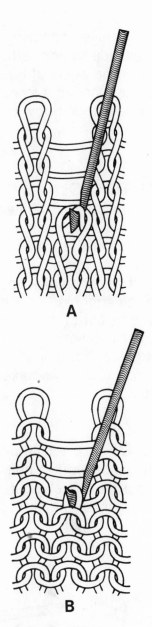

A

B

DROPPED STITCH: To pick up a dropped stitch or correct a mistake, use a crochet hook and pick up the stitch either in Knit (A) or Purl (B).

RIDGE: This raised effect is made on Knit side (Stockinette Stitch) by working a row of Purl, or on Purl side by working a row of Knit. (See color stripes, row B, pg. 118.)

EDGE STITCHES: For a smoother and neater-looking edge, an edge stitch is recommended. The edge stitch also adds a decorative touch when joining seams, and makes it easier to pick up stitches in the armhole.

Knit first and last stitch on every row—this makes a separate edge.

Slip first stitch and Knit last stitch on every row—this makes a thicker edge.

BINDING OFF: The bind off stitches should be worked neither too tightly nor too loosely, but in the same tension as the knitted garment.

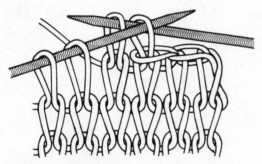

Bind Off in Knit—Work on Knit side.
Step 1. Knit two stitches.
Step 2. With left-hand needle, lift the first stitch over the last worked stitch, as shown above.
Step 3. Knit one more stitch.
Step 4. Repeat step 2.
Repeat steps 3, 4.

Bind Off in Purl—Work on Purl side. Follow same procedure as for Bind Off in Knit, but work in Purl.

Binding off in Knit on Purl side, or in Purl on Knit side creates a decorative ridge.

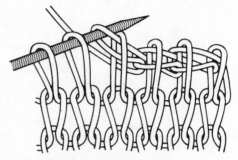

Bind Off in Chain Knit—This is a decorative bind off stitch which has little elasticity. Work on Knit side and in the same tension as garment.
Step 1. Knit two stitches together.
Step 2. Return stitch on right-hand needle to left-hand needle, as shown above.
Repeat steps 1, 2.

Bind Off in Ribbing—Work from either right or wrong side, following the same stitches worked in the rib.

Note: Armhole or neck—When binding off, one stitch will remain on the right-hand needle. This stitch is always counted as part of the following stitches to be worked, thus giving a correct count of stitches on the needle.

Fastening Bind Off Yarn—This prevents a "loopy" last stitch.

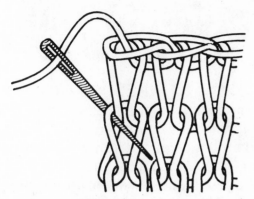

Step 1. Work yarn end through stitch below.

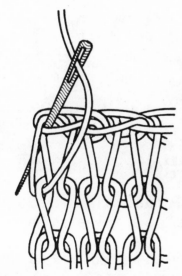

Step 2. Pull yarn firmly and work into last stitch.

Step 3. Weave in yarn end.

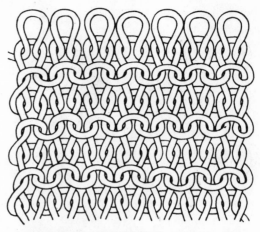

GARTER STITCH: Work every stitch and row in Knit. This creates a ridged effect in every other row. Both sides look the same.

In circular knitting, the Garter Stitch is made by alternating one round of Knit and one round of Purl.

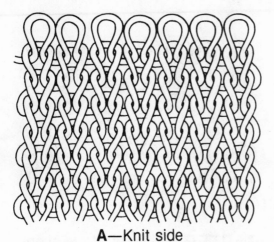

A—Knit side

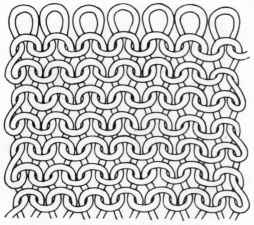

B—Purl side

STOCKINETTE STITCH:

Alternate one row of Knit (right side) and one row of Purl (wrong side). The Knit side has a vertical row effect (A) and the Purl side has a horizontal row effect (B).

In circular knitting, the stitch is made by working all rounds in Knit.

B

A

COLOR STRIPES:

For an even change-over in Stockinette Stitch, work a row of Knit on Knit side (right side) or a row of Purl on Purl side (wrong side), as in A. For a ridged effect, work a row of Purl on Knit side or a row of Knit on Purl side, as in B.

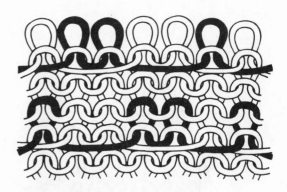

FAIR ISLE KNITTING:

The pattern is achieved by the placement of the different colors, and it is worked in Stockinette Stitch. Method: Change color while working across row. The unused strand is always carried slightly looped across back on the Purl side, as shown above. The color to be worked comes up from under the previously worked color.

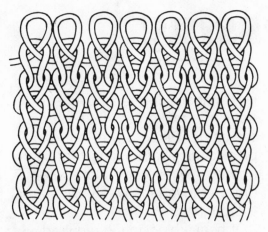

CROSSED STOCKINETTE STITCH:
Alternate one row of Twist Knit with one row of Purl. This adds a decorative effect to "plain" knitting, gives a firmer stitch, and "evens out" uneven knitting in a thin yarn.

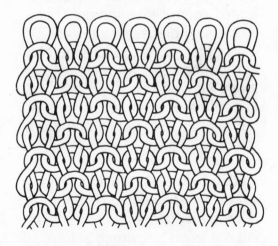

SEED STITCH:
Work a row of Knit and Purl, then a row of Purl and Knit. Knit is worked above Purl and Purl is worked above Knit. Both sides look the same.

This stitch pattern is used as a base for many variations, adding an equal number of Knit and Purl stitches.

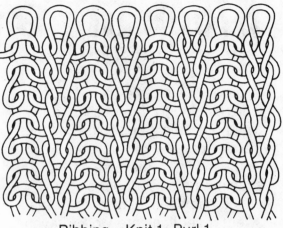

Ribbing—Knit 1, Purl 1

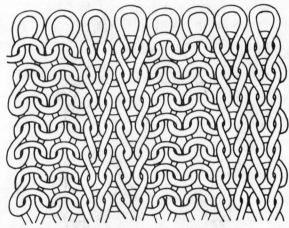

Ribbing—Knit 2, Purl 2

RIBBING:
Combine Knit and Purl stitches in vertical rows. Knit 1, Purl 1, and Knit 2, Purl 2 are the most commonly used. Both sides look the same. Several other stitch combinations are possible as long as they give an elastic effect.

blocking & pressing

In order to keep the hand-knitted look, block only if necessary and avoid pressing if possible. Because the sleeves are knitted directly onto the sweater, the problem of shaping armhole/upper sleeve edges has been eliminated. If the sweater sections are worked evenly, so that pattern stitches and side edges look close to perfect, there is no need to block or press before joining edges.

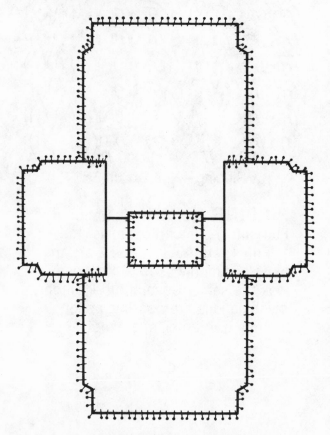

BLOCKING: Place knitted pieces right side up on a well padded soft surface (terry cloth). Pin in place, using rustproof pins. Side and bottom edges should be straight, with sleeves at right angle to the sides.

Measure each section separate-ly. Compare corresponding sections and make sure that they are the same. Place a wet, not dripping, cloth over knitting. Pat lightly and evenly. Remove cloth when dry. Remove pins when sweater is thoroughly dry.

If heavy blocking is required, soak pieces in lukewarm or cold water. Squeeze out excess water by rolling pieces tightly in a terry towel before blocking. For thick yarn that takes a long time to dry, it will be necessary to frequently change the wet towels underneath.

If cleaning is required before blocking, soak pieces in water and a mild soap. Rinse thoroughly before rolling pieces in a towel.

For pieces that require no blocking, but do need a "fresher" look, straighten side edges, place pins in corners only and cover with a damp cloth. Pat gently and leave until dry.

PRESSING: The only places where an iron should be permitted is on the wrong side of seam joinings, and on the wrong side of front bands. An iron must never be used on pattern stitches.

Before pressing a sweater, make a test on the swatch. Place a wet presscloth over the area to be pressed and touch down very lightly with the iron. Never use long, heavy strokes. If the test swatch retains the original "bounce" and appears smoother, go ahead. If the test swatch appears shiny and flattened, avoid pressing altogether.

seam joinings

Join edges either from the right or the wrong side of the garment. When seams are made on the right side, stitches must be neatly worked, and be either decorative or invisible. The stitches should be worked firmly, but not too tightly, for the most professional look.

The advantage of working on the right side, even though a little tricky, is that pattern stitches and color stripes can be matched more easily. If the knitting has been done in an uneven-textured yarn, use a thinner and even-textured yarn in a matching color to join seams.

last stitches of the shoulders correspond, and if possible, use bind off yarn to join seams.

From the right side—Whipstitch together by going through the upper edge of the bind off stitch. For a shoulder seam that won't sag, make a second seam on the wrong side. Whipstitch through the upper, and remaining, edge of the bind off stitch.

From the wrong side—Whipstitch together by going through the lower edge of the bind off stitch. Make a second seam on the same side and Whipstitch through the upper, and remaining, edge of the bind off stitch.

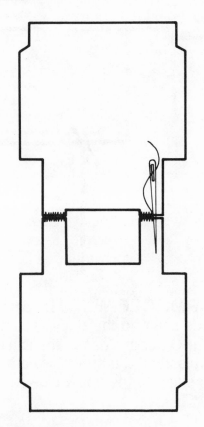

SHOULDERS: With right or wrong sides up, place the Back and Front shoulders opposite each other. Be sure that the first and

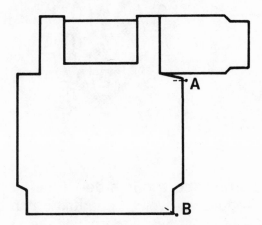

SIDES: With right or wrong sides facing, place the Back and Front pieces together. Join the corresponding top and bottom stitches (A and B). Edges can be joined either by holding the two pieces together, or by placing them edge to edge. Carefully match pattern stitches, and place pins along (or across) the edges before joining the sides. ▷

From right or wrong side—If the edges are worked in Slip Stitch, or worked without separate edge stitches, Whipstitch the edges together.

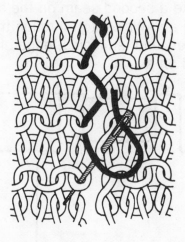

From the wrong side—If the edges are worked in a Knit Stitch, join them by going through the "bumps."

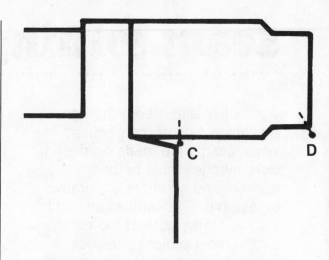

SLEEVES: With right or wrong sides facing, fold the sleeves in half, and join the corresponding stitches at the upper and lower points (C and D). Join the rest of the seam in the same manner as the side seam.

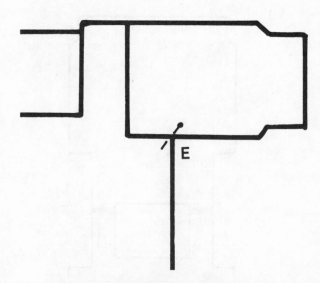

ARMHOLE WIDTH: Join the side seam to the sleeve seam (E). On both sides of the joining, Whipstitch the armhole-width opening to the upper sleeve.

finishings

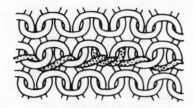

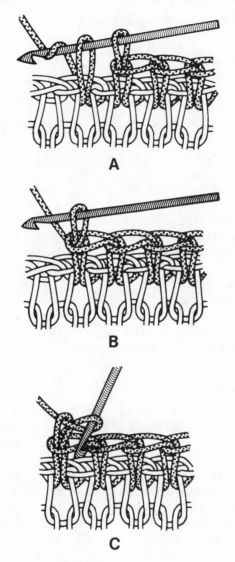

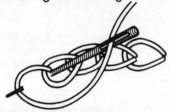

FASTENING YARN ENDS:
After completing each piece, weave in all yarn ends. Thread a tapestry needle and weave in each end on the wrong side. Cut off remaining yarn.
Stripes—Weave ends of each different color into stitches of the same color.
Lace patterns—Avoid carrying a yarn end over an open area.
Knots—Untie any knot and retie in a half square knot, as shown above, before starting to weave in the ends. This prevents a hole from forming on the right side.

CHAIN STITCH: This is the finishing touch for a seam joining, especially useful on a seam for which color stripes had to be matched. (Even if worked carefully, a neat seam joining is still difficult to make.) Select one of the colors used, or choose a contrasting color to work the Chain Stitch.

If the sweater is knitted in an extra-thick or a multi-textured yarn, use a thinner and even-textured yarn to work the stitch. From the right side, begin working in Chain Stitch at the armhole for both side and sleeve seams.

REVERSED SINGLE CROCHET: This is an edge finish. From the right side, work a row of Single Crochet (A and B) along the edge. When working around the neckline, hold the edge (to prevent stretching) by not working between, or into, every knitted stitch. Skip a stitch at even intervals to avoid a puckering effect.

Work the second row of Single Crochet on the same side, but from left to right (C). Cut yarn when completed, and join the first and last stitches together.

index

Page numbers for illustrations are in boldface type.